Exploring Christianity

Christian Life, Personal and Social Issues

Gwyneth Windsor and John Hughes

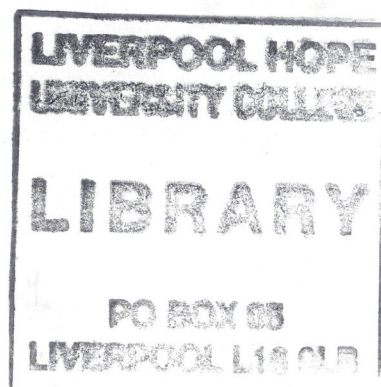

HEINEMANN EDUCATIONAL

Heinemann Educational,
a division of Heinemann Educational Books Ltd,
Halley Court, Jordan Hill, Oxford OX2 8EJ

OXFORD   LONDON   EDINBURGH
MELBOURNE   SYDNEY   AUCKLAND
IBADAN   NAIROBI   GABORONE   HARARE
KINGSTON   PORTSMOUTH N H   (USA)
ATHENS   BOLOGNA   MADRID   SINGAPORE

© Gwyneth Windsor and John Hughes 1991

First published 1991

British Library Cataloguing in Publication Data
Windsor, Gwyneth
  Christian life, personal and social issues.
  1. Christian life
  I. Title   II. Hughes, John   III. Series
  248.4

ISBN 0 435 30272 8 ✓

Designed and produced by VAP Publishing Services, Kidlington, Oxon

Printed and bound in Spain by Mateu Cromo

Acknowledgements

Religious Studies Consultant W. Owen Cole.
Thanks are also due to Roger Owen and Janey Graham for commenting on the manuscript.

The publishers would like to thank the following for permission to reproduce photographs: Mike Abrahams/Network pp. 48 (C), 66 (F); ACE Photo Agency/Richard Walker p. 46 (E); Afrapix/Network p. 60 (B); J. Allan Cash pp. 4 (B), 5 (C), 16 (B), 36 (B), 37 (C), 44 (C), 48 (B), 72 (A); Andes Press Agency p. 12 (B); Arctic Camera/Derek Fordham p. 85 (D); Arkell/Network p. 53 (D); Barnaby's Picture Library pp. 40 (A), 52 (A); The Bridgeman Art Library p. 56 (A); CAFOD p. 77 (B); Camera Press pp. 63 (top left, centre), 80 (A), 88 (A); Canterbury and Rochester Diocesan Council for Social Responsibility p. 41 (C, D); Jacky Chapman/Format Photographers p. 71 (G); Christian Aid p. 77 (A); The Coca-Cola Company p. 60 (A) ('Coca-Cola' and 'Coke' are registered trademarks which identify the same product of The Coca-Cola Company); Colorsport p. 61 (C); Crisis p. 55 (G); Sarah Errington/Hutchison Library p. 89 (top); Robert Francis/Hutchison Library p. 87 (E); Melanie Friend/Format Photographers pp. 62 (D), 71 (F); Ron Gilling/Panos Pictures pp. 51 (E), 54 (E), 82 (D); Mike Goldwater/Network p. 59 (E); Gowan/Network p. 55 (top right); Sally and Richard Greenhill pp. 6 (D), 9 (C), 16 (A), 36 (A), 40 (B), 42 (E), 43 (F), 44 (B), 84 (C), 88 (right); Sonia Halliday Photographs p. 50 (D); Robert Harding Picture Library pp. 48 (A), 80 (B); Paul Harrison/Panos Pictures pp. 56 (B), 89 (B); Jeremy Hartley/Panos Pictures pp. 80 (C), 84 (A); Juliet Highet/Hutchison Library p. 16 (C); Hutchison Library p. 12 (A); Imperial War Museum p. 10 (E); ITC Entertainment Ltd p. 65 (C); Midgley/Greenpeace p. 95 (D); Morgan/Greenpeace p. 67 (G); Joanne O'Brien/Format Photographers p. 70 (D); Raisa Page/Format Photographers p. 70 (D); Tony Pallios/Panos Pictures p. 56 (B); Piel/Frank Spooner Pictures p. 57 (C); Popperfoto pp. 45 (D), 63 (top left), 66 (D), 74 (B), 75 (C); Rex Features pp. 4 (A), 34 (C), 52 (B), 58, 63 (right), 64 (A), 65 (B), 66 (E), 92 (A), 95 (C); Rex Features/Sipa Press/Patrick Frilet p. 94 (B); Carlos Reyes/Andes Press Agency p. 70 (left); Chris Ridgers p. 22 (top left); Barry Searle/Sonia Halliday Photographs p. 33 (A); Shelter p. 54 (F); Alison Sims/Dec McCarthy p. 44 (A); Frank Spooner Pictures/Gamma/Tomkins p. 57 (D); Syndication International Ltd pp. 52 (C), 68 (A, B); Liba Taylor/Hutchison Library p. 84 (B); Topham Picture Source pp. 10 (D), 19 (D), 71 (E); Wigan Record Office p. 39 (D); Young/Network p. 86.

All other photographs supplied by Gwyneth Windsor and John Hughes.

Cover photograph by J. C. Allen

Thanks are also due to the following for permission to reproduce copyright material: Blue Peter for the Blue Peter/Sainsbury's Greenscheme poster p. 94; Mary Castle for the article on p. 62, which appeared in the *Times Educational Supplement*, 16 February 1990; CSV Volunteer Programme for the article p. 5, which appeared in *Adscene*, 10 November 1989; *Daily Mail* for both articles on p. 43, which appeared in the *Daily Mail*, 6 January 1990; Haven Leisure for the extract from their 1990 brochure on p. 47; *Mail on Sunday* for the article on p. 58, which appeared in the *Mail on Sunday*, 18 February 1990.

The publishers have made every effort to contact copyright holders. However, if any material is incorrectly attributed, they would be happy to make the necessary arrangements at the earliest opportunity.

CONTENTS

CARING IS PART OF BEING A PERSON

Reasons for caring for others are often buried deep down in each of us. There are few people who are so selfish or self-centred that they can stand by and see a child suffer. It is part of being a person that most of us have a natural care for others. When we cease to care, we cease to be complete human beings.

THE OLD TESTAMENT VIEWPOINT

In the **Old Testament**, caring for others is an essential part of serving God. People were judged by their love for God, and for other people. 'You shall love the Lord your God' was the first law of **Jewish faith**. 'You shall love your neighbour as much as you love yourself' was the second law. This attitude is still a central part of the Jewish faith.

Care for widows and orphans, considered the most helpless members of the community, was built into the religion. A second picking of an orchard or field of crops was forbidden. Instead, these 'gleanings' were left to be taken by the poorest members of society. Even beggars had their place in the order of Jewish life. It was the duty of good Jews to give to any whose circumstances were worse than their own. Giving to the poor was part of worshipping God. When people became rich with inherited wealth, there was always a temptation to forget God, and the way in which he wanted people to live. There are constant reminders in the Old Testament that God expects a high standard of caring for others. Sometimes the rich forgot to do this. The message of many of the **prophets** was that people should remember to treat others fairly, and with respect.

What God wanted, they were told, was not fancy religious services, but 'to do justly, to love mercy, and to walk humbly with God'. The standard was high, and this has preserved the standards of Jewish behaviour throughout the centuries.

THE NEW TESTAMENT VIEWPOINT

The **New Testament** takes the same sort of view as the Old Testament. There is a constant call to obey God by loving and caring for other people. Jesus seemed to have a special bias towards poor people. He constantly told the rich people that they had to care for the poor. He emphasized that the poor will have a special place in the **Kingdom of Heaven**.

Since the time of **Jesus**, **Christians** have gone on trying to live the ways Jesus wanted them to. Often they have made mistakes, and misunderstood his words. The Christians whom history reckons to be outstanding are those who have shown love for others.

A 'Love your neighbour'

B Christians believe that caring for others is an essential part of serving God

C Caring throughout life

WHY SHOULD I CARE?

The answer is for each individual to work out for themselves. In this book you will find some people who have cared for others in an outstanding way. There are some issues for you to think about, and many unanswered questions. These questions are part of being a person.

NOTES/DATABASE

Look up the following words in the glossary. Then use the definitions to make suitable entries for your notebook or database.

Old Testament   Kingdom of
New Testament   Heaven
Christians   Jesus
Jewish faith   Prophets

Youngsters ease crisis over lack of carers

THEY'RE young, keen, often homesick, and sometimes lonely – but they care about others.

These are the common bonds between youngsters working for Community Service Volunteers.

At any one time, as many as 2,000 young people mostly aged under 24, devote between four months and a year to working on a range of community projects.

Many take time off between leaving school and starting a job or setting off for university or college.

Francis Rooney is one of them. The 21-year-old from Birmingham is spending a year in Sittingbourne, where he is helping to run Swale's Housing Aid and Advice Centre, an initiative funded by the borough council and manned mostly by volunteers.

Francis shares a flat with two youngsters who have recently come out of care. It is a job which demands a high level of dedication. As well as helping them cope with everyday tasks, such as cooking and ironing, Francis also has to provide emotional support.

Like other CSV volunteers all over Britain who help care for mentally and physically handicapped people, the homeless, the young and the elderly, Francis gets just £18.50 a week and his food and expenses paid for.

As well as enjoying helping others, Francis' experience with CSV should help prepare him for his chosen career, either as a social worker or youth worker.

But he does admit to being just a little homesick. "Its been a big culture shock coming down here," he said. "Money goes a lot further in Birmingham – this is such an expensive area."

CSV, which was founded in 1962 and is largely funded by government money, is desperate to recruit more volunteers. "There is a crisis in caring," said Sean Jefferson of CSV. "Thousands of people need support and the professional services alone cannot cope.

"We're very keen for more people to come forward – everyone is accepted because our central philosophy is that everyone has something to offer."

Anyone interested in joining the scheme should contact Donna Miller, at 237 Pentonville Road, London N1, or on 071 278 6601

ACTIVITIES

1 **Quick quiz**

a In which part of the Bible is caring for others an essential part of serving God?

b What is the first law of Jewish life?

c What is the second law of Jewish life?

d Why do you think this attitude is the central part of the Jewish faith?

e How was caring for the most helpless members of the community built into Jewish life?

f What is the duty of every good Jew?

g What was the temptation when people inherited wealth?

h What was the message of the prophets?

i How has the standard of Jewish behaviour been preserved through the centuries?

j What is one way in which the New Testament calls people to obey God?

k Who, according to Jesus, will have a special place in the Kingdom of Heaven?

l Which Christians are often considered to have been important?

Start a scrapbook

2 Start collecting a scrapbook of newspaper cuttings about people who show real care for others. This could be an individual scrapbook, or a class effort.

WHY SHOULD I CARE?

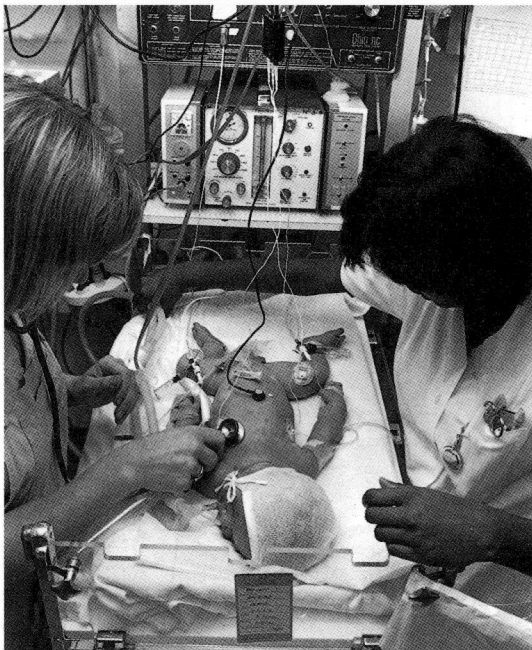

D Some people make caring their profession

WHO IS MY NEIGHBOUR?

'Love your neighbour as much as you love yourself.' Here is a story about loving your neighbour.

Once there was a boy who went to a comprehensive school. His name was David. He got teased a lot by the other children because he had teeth which stuck out. He also talked in a posh accent because he had been brought up to speak like that. David was lucky because he was a whizz kid with computers. He didn't boast about it but it made some of the other children jealous. One day they decided to beat him up . . . again. They went a bit too far this time, and left him on the field unable to move.

When the pips went for afternoon school, they rushed off, leaving him moaning. He called out to them but they did nothing at all. Some other children who knew David came by but they just laughed. Later in the afternoon, some children who were truanting from another school turned up. David was terrified because he knew that the two schools did not get on with each other. He was certain that he would get beaten up again.

To David's amazement, they put a blazer over him to keep him warm and dashed into David's school to find a teacher. They knew they would get into trouble for being out of school. They were prepared to pay that price because they wanted to help someone who was hurt.

1 **Discuss**

If someone asked you who your neighbour was, what answer would you give?

STORYBOARD

1. A man set out on the road between Jerusalem and Jericho.
2. On the way he got mugged. He was left for dead.
3. A priest came past... ...but just ignored him.
4. Then a teacher... ...he ignored him too.
5. But the sales representative stopped and looked after him.
6. Then he took him to the nearest hotel.
7. He left his credit card to pay the bill.
8. Which of these people was a "NEIGHBOUR" to the man who got mugged?

2 Now read the story which Jesus told in Luke 10:25–37.

a What question did the lawyer ask?

b Why do you think he asked that question?

c How did Jesus answer the question?

d What was the real answer to the question?

3 In groups

a Use Jesus' story in Luke 10:25–37, as well as the up-to-date one shown on the left-hand page, to make up your own version of this story. When you have decided on the story, turn it into a play and act it out in your groups. This could make a good presentation for assembly.

b Imagine you are a newspaper reporter. Write the story you used for your play as if it were the front cover story of a newspaper.

THE BACKGROUND TO MOSES' STORY

Originally, the Israelites went to Egypt because there was famine in their own land. They remained there happily until about 1200 BCE when the local population got very worried because there were so many Israelites. Pharaoh, the King of Egypt, decided that he would order the midwives to kill all the boy babies born to Israelite women by throwing them into the Nile. Now look at the film strip on the right to find out what happened to Moses.

PEOPLE WHO CARED – MOSES' MOTHER

IDENTITY CARD

CATEGORY Z: *IMMIGRANT SLAVE*

NAME: Wife of Levi

ADDRESS: Slave quarters, Goshen, Egypt.

Next of Kin: Levi ben Levi

Nationality: Jewish

Status: Slave working in the brickworks

Other Information: Known to be very attached to her children. Will need to be watched carefully. NOT PERMITTED TO LEAVE BRICKWORKS

4 Look at the identity card and read the film strip below. Then answer these questions.

a What were the midwives told to do?

b What do we know about Moses' mother?

c Make a list of ways in which she showed how much she loved her son.

d How did she make sure that her son was found by someone who might be able to take care of him?

e What did Moses' sister do to help?

f What risk did Moses' mother take to make sure her son lived?

g Do you think she acted in a loving way? Write down some reasons for your answer.

THE ADVENTURE OF LIFE

Everyone starts out on the great adventure of life by being born into a family. Sometimes other circumstances may mean that the child has to live in a foster family, or occasionally in a hospital or home. Some children may be part of a family with two parents while others will be part of a single parent family. Many will have brothers and sisters. Whatever the circumstances, the adventure begins with a child living in a community with other people, and gradually discovering their own and other people's identities.

REGISTRATION

In the UK, all children must be **registered** within six weeks of their birth (or three weeks in Scotland). This means that their parents have to go to the local **register office** and fill in forms which give basic information about the new baby. The parents will have been given a certificate by the hospital where the baby was born, or by the midwife or doctor who attended the birth. This is proof that the new baby has arrived. They take this to the **registrar**. He or she then puts the baby's name on the official list of all the people in the country, and gives the new child a **birth certificate**.

PRIVILEGES OF CITIZENSHIP

As soon as a child is registered in the UK, he or she has certain rights and privileges. Children of British **citizens** are automatically British citizens themselves, and have the right of the full protection of British Law. The mothers can claim **child benefit** for the new baby. This is a sum of money paid each week, to help towards the costs of bringing up a child. If parents are unemployed, then the families receive extra money from the Department of Social Security to try to make sure that the child can be adequately looked after. Children also have the right to have a passport of their own, so that they may, if the parents wish it, travel abroad.

B Passports

A What does it mean to be registered as a citizen?

RIGHTS OF THE CHILD

According to law in Britain, parents have certain duties towards their children. As well as registering the child's birth, parents have to obey the law which says that children must be educated. Usually this means that parents must make sure their children go to school. Parents are also expected to provide their children with a home, food and appropriate health care. Neglecting or abusing a child is against the law, and parents who do this can be punished.

IMPORTANCE OF PARENTS

Parents give children their first experience of human love and care. They are the people who set the standards of behaviour and of love which a child will accept as normal. Like all human beings, children are looking for love, and the natural place to find it is at home. The people who care for a child in his or her early years have an enormous responsibility. The impression they leave on a child will influence him or her throughout life.

C Children should learn about caring

Here is some advice which St Paul (whose letters are in the Christian Bible), gave to parents and children:

"Parents: do not treat your children in such a way as to make them angry. Instead, bring them up with Christian discipline and instruction.
Parents: do not irritate your children, or they will become discouraged".

"Children: it is your Christian duty to obey your parents, for this is the right thing to do. Respect your father and mother is the first commandment."

NOTES/DATABASE

Look up the following words in the glossary. Then use the definitions to make suitable entries for your notebook or database.

Register   Citizen
Birth certificate Register office
Registrar   Child benefit

ACTIVITIES

1 Quick quiz

a How does everyone start out on the great adventure of life?

b Name two kinds of family.

c What other kinds of community might a child live in?

d When must new babies be registered?

e What do the parents have to do when a new baby is registered?

f What does every child receive when he or she is registered?

g When does a child become a British citizen?

h What rights does a child in the UK have?

i What duties do parents have towards their children?

j What advice does Paul give parents?

k What advice does Paul give children?

ADVICE FROM AROUND THE WORLD

One wise son will make his father glad. Forty fools are no use to him. (Hindu saying)
Children should never cause anxiety to their parents except by unavoidable illness. (Confucius)
Be good to your parents. (The Qur'ān)

He who honours his father shall have joy from his own children. (Ecclesiastes)
He who spares the rod hates his own son. (Proverbs)
Children, it is your Christian duty to obey your parents. Parents, do not treat your children in such a way as to make them angry. (Paul)

2 Read the quotations shown above. They are advice to parents from a number of different world religions.

a Draw a chart like the one shown below. Now put the advice from around the world into your own idea of the order of importance. You may find it useful to do this in groups so that you can discuss each piece of advice.

b Choose *one* piece of advice, and explain what you think it really means by giving some examples.

c Now make up your own piece of good advice to parents. Where would you place it in order of importance?

Order	Advice	Source

FURTHER ACTIVITIES

SOME OTHER ATTITUDES TO CHILDREN

A Sparta

In Sparta, in ancient Greece, babies who looked sickly or mis-shapen or simply ugly were not allowed to live. They were left exposed on the mountains to die. At the age of seven, all boys were taken from their parents, and brought up by the State. They were then drilled and trained to become tough soldiers. This was for the good of the Spartan State which considered it very important to have good soldiers. Some of the rules were a bit surprising. If the boys were caught stealing, they were beaten. The beating was not for stealing but for being clumsy enough to get caught.

B Russia 1917–1935

After the Russian Revolution, children in Russia were encouraged to join groups for young communists, and to give up some of their free time to serving the State as 'Young Pioneers'.

C Hitler Youth

In Hitler's Germany earlier this century, young people were trained to complete obedience. They were educated to be loyal to the State rather than to their own parents. They were encouraged to report family and friends to the police if they thought they were being disloyal to Germany. Some of the young people did so, and saw their friends and families taken away to almost certain death in concentration camps.

D Young Pioneers

E The Hitler Youth put the State before families

In each of these ideas which we find in history, what was being considered was the good of the State rather than the welfare or individuality of the child.

1 Discuss

Do you think there could ever be a time when the good of the whole country was more important than the welfare of the children?

PARENTS

How long do parents need to guide and protect their children?

Babies and small children are obviously helpless creatures who need daily care, protection and guidance. This goes on for many years. But just how many years? There comes a time when children want to be independent. Sometimes parents think that their children try to be independent too early.

2 a Conduct a class survey to find out how many people feel that their parents are too fussy.

Survey Form

Do your parents have rules about:

a) bringing friends home;	Yes/No
b) walking home with other people;	Yes/No
c) doing homework;	Yes/No
d) going out in the evening;	Yes/No
e) going out at weekends;	Yes/No
f) the time you get in at night;	Yes/No
g) the places you go to when you go out with friends;	Yes/No

Do you break their rules:
Sometimes/Often/Seldom/Never

Do your friends ever laugh at the rules your parents impose? Yes/No

Do you think the rules your parents make are stricter than those of your friends' parents? Yes/No

Do you think the rules are necessary? Yes/No

What would you like to see changed about the way your parents treat you?

....
....
....

b Make sure you collect the results of your survey and display them in a way which is easy to understand. This could be by producing bar charts and then writing a conclusion when you have seen the results of your survey.

THE FATHER WHO WENT ON WAITING

One day I was sorting out old papers in the attic and I found a diary. It was written by my father...

Today my son asked me for the money he would inherit when I die. I was shocked. I hope I've a good few years left yet.

I decided to give my son the money and he has gone off thinking he'll never return. Now I must begin the long wait until he returns. The older boy has taken it very well and is working hard.

Still no word from the lad. I wonder what he is doing.

I can't help worrying about the boy...

Can't seem to get Jimmy out of my mind ...still, Henry is working very hard.

Jimmy's been gone a year now. But I'm certain he'll be back soon.

I'm always looking along the road to see if he is coming. There will be a real feast when he gets back...

PEOPLE WHO CARED— THOMAS BARNADO

Thomas Barnado, who was born in Dublin in 1845, wanted to be a medical missionary in China. That was why he went to train as a doctor at the London Hospital in the East End of London.

The poverty of the East End of London was a shock to Thomas Barnado. With some other Christian students, he started some 'ragged schools'. At first he did not realize the awful conditions under which some of the boys lived. Some lived with their families in overcrowded rooms scraping a living by doing 'piece work' for factories. Some had started to live on the streets, under tarpaulins and with whatever shelter they could find. Sometimes these boys would huddle together on a roof, clinging to the chimney pots to try and keep warm.

Barnado realized that he was needed to help these boys in the East End. He did not go to China but instead began refuges for homeless and destitute boys.

One night, a ginger-headed boy called John Somers wanted to stay in the hostel but Barnado turned him away because he had no room. That night, the boy froze to death. After that, Barnado put up a sign. It said, 'No destitute child ever refused admission'.

3 a Now read Luke 15:11–32 and finish the story for yourself. Make sure you describe carefully how you think the father felt when his son returned.

b If you were ever missing for a long time, how do you think your parents would feel about it?

FACT FILE

Admissions to Barnado's in 1888
1044 – aged over 12
547 – aged 6–12
505 – no parents
777 – no father
196 – both parents had run off, leaving children on the streets.

4 What reasons can you think of for children being in care today?
In what ways are the reasons for them being in care different from the reasons for admissions to Barnardo's a hundred years earlier?

When a Christian couple decide they want to be husband and wife they usually choose to get married in a church. Like any couple, they plan their marriage carefully. The church in which they marry is often the church which they attend each week on Sunday. They are therefore already part of the wider church family. The Christians in the church will continue to support and help them as they begin their married life.

A

PREPARATION FOR MARRIAGE

Many churches help people to prepare for marriage through a series of meetings. Sometimes, these involve older married couples who try to prepare the couple for the difficulties as well as the joys

ahead. They encourage them to think through the problems of housing and money, and of simply coping with having another person around. Usually there is a meeting with the minister or **priest** who will officiate at the wedding. He or she will want to know about the couple's own hopes and fears, for the whole of life as well as for the marriage. This is an opportunity for the couple to think about their own religious beliefs, and to sort out in their own minds what they believe about God. Many Christian couples use their wedding as a chance to dedicate their lives to God as a pair.

The preparation for marriage also includes planning the service. Roman Catholic couples can look forward to a special service, called a **Nuptial Mass** as part of their wedding celebrations. The **Mass** is the most important part of worship for Roman Catholics. During the service, the **Last Supper** which Jesus had with his disciples is re-enacted when the people eat bread and wine in remembrance that Jesus died for everyone who believes in him. As this is the central part of Roman Catholic worship, it is not surprising that Roman Catholic couples should wish this to be a part of their wedding. Like other Christians in the Western part of the world, the bride usually likes to wear white on her wedding day. It is the symbol of purity, as well as the Church's colour for specially joyful festivals.

PROMISES

Christian marriages include the exchange of promises. The man and woman each promise that they will go on loving and caring for each other throughout their lives. A symbol of these promises is the wedding ring. In Eastern Orthodox churches the central feature of the marriage is the crowning of the bride.

The most important people at a marriage service are the bride and the

B

groom (the special words for the woman and the man). The priest or minister is there to act as a sort of Master of Ceremonies, and also to bless the couple as they start their married life together.

Although some Anglicans also include Holy Communion in the wedding ceremony it is less common than in the Roman Catholic Church. Weddings are joyful occasions. There is a tradition of church choirs singing special hymns for the service. As bride and groom pose for photographs, bells often peal out from the church tower telling everyone the good news that there has been a wedding.

PATTERN OF THE CEREMONY

The pattern of marriage is similar in each of the churches. The bride is 'given away' by her father, or another close relative. Traditionally she then passes into the care of her new husband. The minister or priest makes sure that the couple actually want to get married, by asking questions. He or she also makes sure that they are free to get married to each other. After a series of promises, rings are exchanged, prayers are said for the new marriage, and a blessing given.

It is a legal requirement that a marriage register is kept and that it is signed by the bride and the groom, the minister or registrar who officiated, and also by two witnesses.

SACRAMENTAL ACT

Some Christians believe that marriage is a **sacrament**. This means that it is a symbolic religious act in which God plays his part just as much as the man and woman involved. They believe that God has a perfect plan for everyone's life, and that he guides people into marrying the right person. With his help, the marriage is a permanent relationship which God himself has planned.

Amongst the groups who take this view are Roman Catholics. As they believe that marriages are planned by God, it makes it difficult for them to accept divorce, and in fact the Roman Catholic Church accepts divorce only on rare occasions. Anglicans accept divorce and it is now possible to be remarried after divorce in the Church of England. Other denominations, like the Methodists and the United Reformed Church, do not consider marriage a sacrament. The question of remarriage in church is therefore easier for them, and ministers readily remarry divorced people if they feel it is right to do so.

"Friends, I take this my Friend ..., to be my husband promising through Divine assistance to be unto him a loving and faithful wife, so long as we both on earth shall live."

(From a Meeting for Worship after a Quaker wedding)

NOTES/DATABASE

Look up the following words in the glossary. Then use the definitions to make suitable entries for your notebook or database.

Priest	Last Supper
Mass	Sacrament
Nuptial Mass	Covenant

ACTIVITIES

1 Quick quiz

a Where do many Christian couples decide to get married?

b Who will continue to support the couple as they start married life together?

c How do some churches help couples prepare for marriage?

d What kinds of problems are the couple encouraged to think about?

e Why do the couple usually meet the priest or minister who will marry them before the ceremony?

f What other preparations for the marriage are there?

g Which special service do many Roman Catholics have as part of their wedding celebrations?

h Why is the Nuptial Mass important to Roman Catholics?

i What is the reason for brides wearing white at their wedding?

j What symbol is used to remind the bride and groom of the promises they have made to each other?

k What is the role of the minister or priest at the wedding?

l What is the meaning behind the bride being 'given away' by a close relative?

m What is the legal requirement at a marriage?

n What do some Christians believe about God's part in their marriage?

o Why does this make it more difficult for these Christians to accept the idea of divorce?

p Why do some of the Reformed churches, such as the United Reformed Church, find it easier to accept the idea of remarrying divorced people?

2 Look carefully at the pictures on this page.

a What do they tell you?

b In your books record the letter of the picture against the correct caption.

(i) A Greek Orthodox wedding.

(ii) The wedding ring is a symbol of all types of Christian marriage.

FURTHER ACTIVITIES

Engagements/Weddings

Houghton/Wright

Both families are pleased to announce the engagement of Mr William Wright, only son of Mr John and Mrs Sarah Wright, to Lucy Houghton, second daughter of Mr Geoff and Mrs Rosemary Houghton, on 11 February 1990.

Faulkner/Clare

Congratulations to Bruce and Helen on

The announcement of marriages is the announcement of agreements between people. The Bible has a special word for agreement. It is *covenant*. A covenant is an agreement in which one person says, 'If you do this, then I will do that.' It is based on trust between the two sides that they will each stick to what they have promised. What do you think the two sides promise in a marriage?

1 Copy and complete the following chart, filling in your own ideas about the two sides of the marriage covenant.

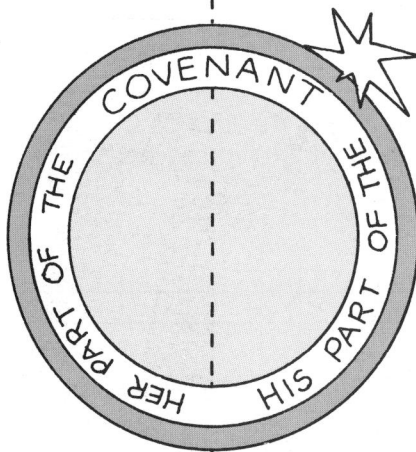

Remember, a covenant is an *equal* partnership!

THE FISHERMAN'S ADVICE

2 Read carefully 1 Peter 3:1–7. The person who probably wrote this was Peter, a very close friend of Jesus. Here is a profile of Peter.

a Make a list of the parts of Peter's advice which you think are good.

b Discuss whether there are any parts of Peter's advice which you disagree with. In which ways would your advice to husbands and wives differ from that of Peter?

c Do you think Peter saw marriage as an equal partnership? Are there any particular words in his advice which make you answer in this way?

d Use the profile of Peter to help you work out some reasons why Peter gave this advice.

NAME: Simon bar Jonah (Nicknamed Peter, meaning the Rock, by Jesus of Nazareth)

DATE OF BIRTH: about 6 BCE

PLACE OF BIRTH: Capernaum in Galilee, Northern Judea

RELIGIOUS AFFILIATION: Originally a Jew. Became a close friend and follower of Jesus of Nazareth. After the death of Jesus, he became one of the leaders of the group known as Christians. He was one of the first to allow Gentiles (non-Jews) to be baptized as Christians. Peter later moved to Rome, where it is thought he became a leader amongst this group called Christians. It is believed that when the Roman Emperor Nero began to persecute Christians, Peter was executed by being crucified upside down. His crime was being a follower of Jesus of Nazareth.

'MOST PEOPLE NOWADAYS TAKE MARRIAGE TOO LIGHTLY'

3 Interpreting the statistics
Look carefully at the chart.

a In which two groups of people surveyed did the largest numbers think that most people now take marriage too lightly?

b Can you think of any reason for the other two groups taking a less serious view of marriage? Write down your reasons.

c Add together the percentages of people holding each opinion. Now create a new bar chart or pie chart for the total numbers. What does this tell you?

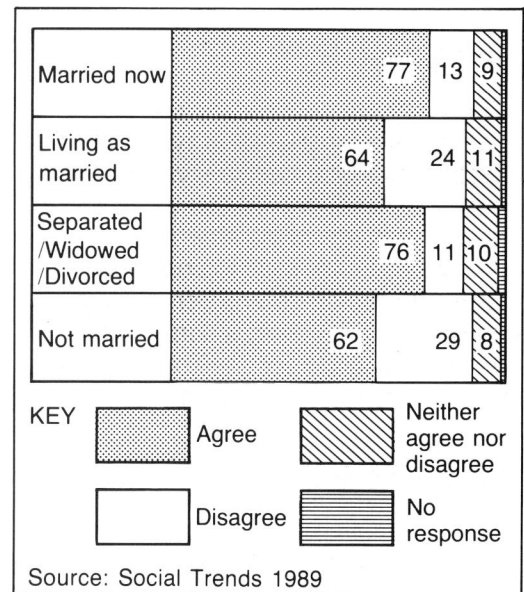

d How would you respond to the statement 'Most people nowadays take marriage too lightly'?

	Agree	Disagree	Neither agree nor disagree	No response
Married now	77	13	9	
Living as married	64	24	11	
Separated /Widowed /Divorced	76	11	10	
Not married	62	29	8	

KEY: Agree / Disagree / Neither agree nor disagree / No response

Source: Social Trends 1989

TWO DIFFERENT WAYS OF LOOKING AT MARRIAGE

1 + 1 = MONOGAMY
That means having only one partner. *This can be an equal partnership.*

1 + M + A + N + Y = POLYGAMY
That means having many partners, usually one husband and several wives.
This usually means someone has to be boss!

MARRIAGE IN THE OLD TESTAMENT

The type of marriage depends on the type of society. The Bible has several different patterns of marriage. In the Old Testament **polygamy** was the usual kind of marriage (if you could afford it!) By New Testament times, Timothy recommends that leaders of the Church should have only one wife.

POLYGAMY

On the right is an example of polygamy. In the early days of the Old Testament, many people were nomads. They went from place to place in search of pasture for their animals. Life was hard, and more wives meant more children to help with the work, so polygamy was the usual form of marriage. This is still the way of life in some places today.

To find out what happened next, read Genesis 38–44.

Jacob had two wives

Leah

who had TEN sons

and Rachel
who had only two sons,   Joseph and Benjamin.

Jacob loved Rachel most,
and Joseph reminded him of her.

Hi! look at ME!

SO
He spoiled the boy.

The marriage service helps the couple to feel committed to one another. It also helps society to see the couple as a new social unit, a family. Some people still find it easier to relate to two people who have made the public commitment of marriage than to two people who have decided to live together.

A A new beginning

A NEW BEGINNING

A marriage is a new beginning. When Jesus was asked about marriage, he pointed back to the beginning of the Bible. He said that in marriage, two people left the protection of their parents to become a new social unit.

Although some Christians give the impression that sex is a forbidden subject, this was not Jesus' attitude. He taught that love and lust are two very different things and that marriage should always be based on love. The sex act is the expression of deep and intimate love between two people. Marriage, according to Jesus, can and should be permanent. 'Don't let anyone separate what God has joined together' was his advice.

Christians see marriage as a symbolic religious act undertaken by two people in the presence of God. In societies where people select their own marriage partners, they have a responsibility to find out enough about each other to feel sure that their relationship will become strong enough to cope with any of the problems which they will meet.

When two people begin the commitment of married life, their relationship needs to be deepened. Sex is one of the ways that this is accomplished. It is both the expression of their love, and the means of strengthening their relationship. They will then be able to provide the kind of loving environment necessary for the children which are the hope of many Christian marriages. It is the intention of the Christian Church that children should be conceived in love and brought into a home where there is a loving relationship in which they can share.

Christians see marriage as a lifelong commitment to one another. This includes being loved in old age by one's partner, as well as by the children of the partnership.

B Christians believe that marriage is a lifelong commitment

SOME ALTERNATIVES TO MARRIAGE

Casual sex: this view says enjoy, without commitment. It is a less popular view now than a few years ago, since the AIDS virus has made us think much about the physical dangers of casual sex. Christians believe that the sexual act is so important, and so central to a loving relationship that it is devalued by casual sex.

Living together: historically, there have been some interesting customs relating to living together. **Handfasting** was common until the 19th century in both Scotland and Denmark. Two people were publicly handfasted and agreed to live together on a trial basis for a year and a day. At the end of that time, either a marriage took place or they were both free. If, however, there were any children, they had to be supported by the person who objected to the marriage.

In the West Indies, it was common for two people who were committed to one another to live together until they could afford a grand wedding. This was often some years later.

Some people now choose to live together instead of getting married. In some cases this is intended to be a permanent arrangement. In others, it is to see how the arrangement will work, which can cause a great deal of hurt if the couple separate.

Christians understand the couples who make a lifelong commitment to one another without choosing to be married. However, Christian couples need the

C Marriage customs vary around the world

fellowship and support of other Christians throughout their marriage. They therefore prefer to make their promises to one another in a public ceremony and to receive the prayers of fellow Christians for their lives together.

MARRIAGE CUSTOMS IN THE OLD TESTAMENT

Marriages were arranged by parents. It was the duty of everyone to get married. There was little social contact between the sexes prior to marriage. The bride had to be paid for because she would work in her husband's household.

There was a formal betrothal, which was probably the first time the two had met. Then, on the wedding day, the bridegroom and his friends came along tc collect the bride. The couple were escorted back through the village to the husband's home. The invited guests lined the route with torches. Then the feasting began . . . and often went on for a week.

NOTES/DATABASE

Look up the following word in the glossary. Then use the definition to make a suitable entry for your notebook or database.

Handfasting

2 What is really important?

What qualities do you think are important in a partner?

Write down the qualities in the order of importance to *you*. (There is no right answer to this.) Add any other factors which you think are important.

ACTIVITIES

1 Quick quiz

a How does the marriage ceremony help the couple who are getting married?

b How does the marriage ceremony help the society?

c Why do you think that some people find it easier to relate to a couple who are married than to a couple who are living together?

d Write *three* sentences about Jesus' teaching on marriage.

e Write down *one* way in which Christians view marriage.

f Write down *one* reason why couples planning to get married need to find out a great deal about each other (in societies where people choose their own marriage partner).

g What is *one* of the ways in which the relationship is deepened within a marriage?

h How does this help to provide a loving environment for the children?

i How long are Christian marriages intended to last?

j Why are Christians not in favour of casual sex?

k Describe what was meant by *handfasting*.

MARRIAGE . . . A BEGINNING

FURTHER ACTIVITIES

	Book of Common Prayer 1662	Alternative Service Book 1980	My own order of importance
	1. To have children	1. Companionship	
	2. Sex	2. Sex	
	3. Companionship	3. To have children, if they want to.	

WHY GET MARRIED?

1 The Church of England gives three reasons for getting married in the introduction to the marriage service.

a In what way has the order changed since the 17th century?

b What reasons can you think of for this change in the order of importance?

c Fill in the final column of the chart with your own order of importance.

WHAT THE MEDIA TELLS US!

2 How is marriage presented on TV?

Watch an English 'soap' and one from another country which involves some married couples.

a Now design a report sheet similar to the one on the right. You will probably think of many different questions. (You could use a word processor and desk top publishing system to do this if either is available.) Fill in a report for each of the programmes you watch.

b Now answer these questions:

(i) What are the main differences between the English soap and the other one?

Name of programme	
Names of married couples	1.
	2.
	3.
Did any of the couples show that they cared about each other? How many quarrels were there during this episode?	
How many of the couples have broken marriages? How many unhappy people were there in this episode?	
How many people are being unfaithful? How many children are suffering as a result of their parents' behaviour?	

(ii) How true to real life do you think each programme was?

(iii) How similar do you think the marriages shown on TV are to Jesus' view on marriage? (Look back to the previous spread to remind yourself about Jesus' attitude to marriage.)

A JOB FOR LIFE

3 Marriage has been called the most difficult job anyone will ever do. Difficult jobs usually require a lot of training.

a Do you think you need any special training for marriage?

b What training have most people had?

c How do most people learn about marriage?

TYPES OF TRAINING

4 a Using the diagram on the right, show the type of training that occurs in the places named.

b What other sorts of training do you think might be helpful in preparing people for the most important job of their lives?

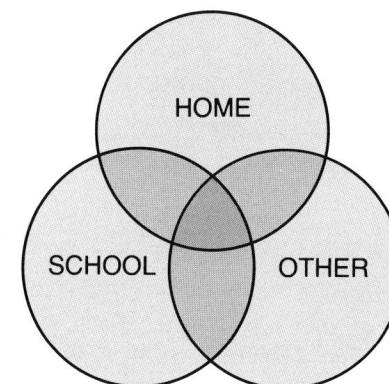

HOME

SCHOOL   OTHER

FOUR KINDS OF LOVE

The New Testament was written in Greek. There are four different words for *love* in Greek.

(i) *Agape* is the kind of love which comes from deep down inside the person. It is constant loving and caring. For example, the kind of love which made it possible for Mother Teresa to go on caring for sick and dying people in Calcutta.

(ii) *Störge* is affection between parents and children, brothers and sisters.

(iii) *Fileos* is the kind of love we have for our closest friends. It is a kind of comfortable companionship with people of either sex.

(iv) *Eros* is the word for sexual love. This kind of love is a reactive love and needs a response in the other person to be complete.

---

5 Discuss

How can each of these kinds of love find expression within Christian marriage?

Think about the people you love and care about. Which type of love do you have for each of them?

A MARRIAGE HAS BEEN ARRANGED . . .

6 Read Genesis 24.

Abraham had been away from his native land for many years. When his son Isaac was old enough to be married, Abraham wanted him to marry a girl from his own country rather than one from the area in which they were then living. (Gen. 24:1–4)

a What reason can you think of for Abraham wanting Isaac to marry someone of his own nationality?

b Who chose the girl?

c How did he make sure she was suitable?

d Was she willing to marry Isaac?

"What the lad needs is a nice girl from back home!"

---

7 Discuss

a How similar do you think today's reasons for arranged marriages are to those of Abraham?

b Arranged marriages are less likely to end in divorce. What reasons can you think of for this?

---

8 Drama

Look at the description of Old Testament marriage customs on the previous spread. This could come alive if you act it out.

First of all, design a storyboard which shows clearly the order of events. This will help you organize the action more easily.

Now divide the class into the bride's friends and relations and the groom's friends and relations. Decide who will take the principal parts. If you want to dress up, look at some pictures of clothes in Bible times. The bride's head-dress is important. It has a number of gold coins hanging over her forehead. You might like to try making one of these.

D Mother Teresa showed a special kind of love for the people she worked among

THE WORLDWIDE CHRISTIAN FAMILY

Christians think of themselves as part of a worldwide Christian family. They believe:

1 that God created everything and therefore he is 'father' to everyone in the world.

2 that God is 'father' in a special way, to those people who believe in Jesus. People who believe in Jesus are called Christians. They call themselves the Christian family or **Church**. This means that Christians expect to treat other people, and especially other Christians, as brothers and sisters, because God is the father of them all.

CHRISTIAN FAMILIES

Everyone belongs to a family. Each smaller Christian family belongs to a wider network of Christian families which make up their local church. This is how it works:

All the families in a local church will try to support and help each other. They also try to include in their activities people who have chosen to remain single, as well as young unmarried people. Many church activities are centred around the family and this helps them to join together. They can worship together at family services, spend weekends away together, join in parish lunches and attend mother and toddler clubs. Many Christian families extend their family by including lonely people or perhaps by fostering a child who has to live apart from his or her own parents. Offering hospitality to people is thought of as a 'gift'. It is as important to have this gift as to be able to teach, to heal or preach sermons. (Romans 12:13)

FAMILY PATTERNS

Christian families follow the same pattern as other families in the same society. **Monogamy**, or being married to one partner only, is the usual rule.

In the Western world, most Christian families now are 'nuclear families'. This means that the parents and their children live as an independent group. They still keep in touch with grandparents, uncles and aunts and other relations, but live in a separate house, often some distance from other relatives.

'Extended families' are more usual in some countries. An extended family is one in which several generations of relations live in one household. Of course, those people who live in a nuclear family also have an extended family. Sometimes, when elderly relatives need to be cared for, they return to live with younger relations.

Worldwide Christian family.
Local Christian family or church.
Individual Christian family.

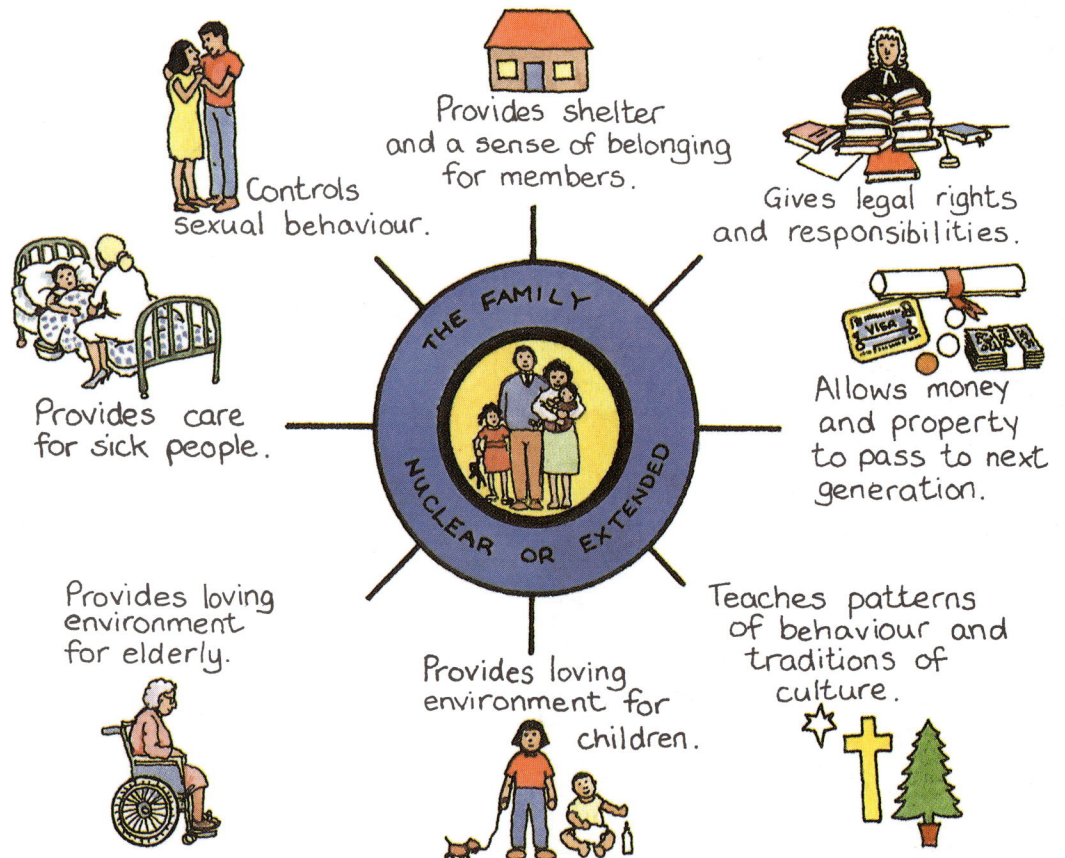

SOME FUNCTIONS OF A FAMILY

Controls sexual behaviour.

Provides shelter and a sense of belonging for members.

Gives legal rights and responsibilities.

Provides care for sick people.

THE FAMILY NUCLEAR OR EXTENDED

Allows money and property to pass to next generation.

Provides loving environment for elderly.

Provides loving environment for children.

Teaches patterns of behaviour and traditions of culture.

WHAT IS A FAMILY FOR?

It is intended that the family provides a stable background. It helps people cope with problems. It prepares children for adult life. In the family children are taught the ways in which society expects them to behave. This is called 'socialization'.

A family should cater for the needs of all its members. This includes bringing up children and looking after their spiritual and emotional needs as well as their physical needs. Married adults hope to find sexual satisfaction which deepens their relationship. A strong relationship between the married adults results in a more loving environment for the children. This means that everyone is able to develop their own talents and interests and to find their place both in the family and in society.

WHEN THINGS GO WRONG

Ideally a family provides support for all its members. Sadly, things can go badly wrong. When this happens it is often the children who suffer most. Family frustrations are sometimes taken out on the children. This can result in child abuse, especially when the adults involved were abused as children themselves. The abuse may take the form of physical violence, physical and emotional neglect, or sometimes emotional and sexual abuse.

NOTES/DATABASE

Look up the following words in the glossary. Then use the definitions to make suitable entries for your notebook or database.

Church   Monogamy

ACTIVITIES

1 Quick quiz

a Explain why Christians think of themselves as part of the Christian family called the Church.

b What is one way in which the New Testament refers to the Christian family?

c What difference do you think it makes to your attitude to people in other countries if you regard them as brothers and sisters?

d How does the Church try to encourage families to do things together?

e Describe what is meant by a nuclear family.

f What is meant by an extended family?

g How does a family help people cope with the practical problems of everyday living?

h How are relationships between married adults deepened?

i Who are the people most likely to be hurt when problems occur in a family?

j What kinds of abuse may happen to children?

2 Family roles

We have a snippet of information about Jesus and his family in Luke 2:41–52. This tells about a family journey to Jerusalem when Jesus was 12 years old. The lad went off on his own, and caused his parents a great deal of worry. They had to leave the rest of their party on the return journey to go to look for him. After this escapade, Jesus was obedient to his parents.

Later, it seems, Joseph died. Matthew 12:47ff speaks of Jesus' mother and brothers, but not his father.

It would seem that Jesus' family was a typical Jewish family in which older people, especially, were honoured and in which it was the duty of the eldest son to enter the same profession as his father. In Jesus' case, this was carpentry. As the eldest son, his role may well have included the responsibility of looking after younger children, as well as providing for the family after the death of his father.

What roles did Jesus have within his family?

3 Draw this chart and state the roles taken by each of the members of your family.

Person	Responsibilities	Privileges

FAMILY MATTERS

FURTHER ACTIVITIES

THE BIBLICAL VIEWPOINT

Luke 2:39

Jesus grew up in a family

Deuteronomy 6:4–7

Children are taught about God in the family

Mark 10: 6–9

Family life created by God.

Jesus saw it as basis of society

Good News Bible

Illustrated

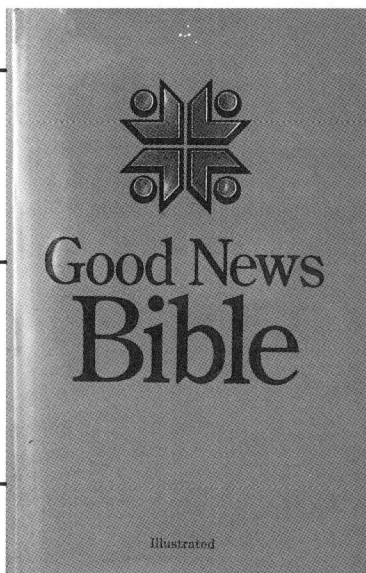

Deuteronomy 25: 5–6

Laws protected older family members

Deuteronomy 24:5

Special privileges given to newly weds to help them become an established social unit.

1 Timothy 5:8

Families must love each other

Ephesians 6:1–4

Obligations for parents and children

FAMILY PRIDE

3 a Look up Philippians 3:5–7. Why was Paul proud of his family background?

b Now look at Philippians 3:8–11. What does Paul think is more important than a good family background?

IDENTITY CARD

NAME SAUL OF TARSUS

TRIBE BENJAMIN

RACE JEW

PROFESSION TENTMAKER

STUDYING RELIGION

Issued by

UNIVERSITY OF TARSUS

FAMILY TREES

4 Knowing your ancestors was important in Biblical times. Mary and Joseph knew that they were descendants of King David. This was why they had to return to Bethlehem for the census. Bethlehem was the home town for everyone who was a descendant of King David. Look at Luke 3:23–37 to see Jesus' family tree.

Now see if you can work out your own family tree. You may need the help of older relatives to do this.

IRENE — ROLAND

HETTY — JOHN — ROLAND — PHYLLIS

CAROL

RALPH — RACHEL — ANDREW

JOHN — EMMA — ME

You *choose* your friends... you are *stuck* with your family.

I like to have a family because I want to feel that I belong somewhere.

1 Imagine you made one of the statements above. Write about the reasons someone might have had for making that particular statement.

THREE ELEMENTS IN FAMILY LIFE

2 Copy and complete the chart by filling in the ways you receive each of the above elements of family life.

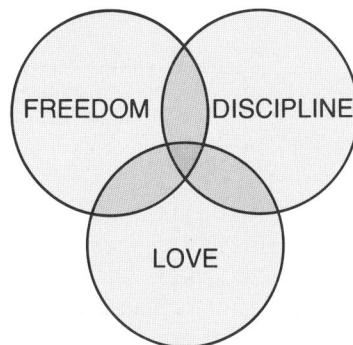

FREEDOM   DISCIPLINE

LOVE

THEN AND NOW

5 Look at the chart. In the left-hand column are some elements of family life in biblical times. Copy the chart. Complete it by filling in the right-hand column with equivalent or alternative elements which apply to family life today.

Then	Now	Then	Now
Agricultural		Everyone knew their place in the family	
Extended family		Spiritual life centred on the home	
Distant members lived near		Faith important	
No generation gap		Children obeyed parents	
Respect for age and wisdom		Parents instructed children in faith	
Traditions important		Faith part of family atmosphere and heritage	
Children "seen and not heard"			
Refuge from world			

FAMILY CYCLE

6 Look at the illustration of a family cycle, on the right. Which households do you know which fit into each stage of the picture?

FAMILY CYCLE

① Young couple. Both working. No children.

② Young couple with children.

③ Older couple. Children leaving

Knock on Grandma's door!

④ Older couple. Children independent.

⑤ Only one remaining partner.

LEARNING SKILLS

7 Where do you learn your skills? Copy the following chart, placing a tick in the appropriate column

Skill	Home and family	School	Other
Mix with people			
Speak clearly			
Sort out personal problems			
Play musical instrument			
Play games			
Make own decisions			
Think about a career			
Use library			
Drive a car			
Form a political opinion			
Paint a house			
Cook a family meal			
Service a car			
Clean a loo			
Gardening			

8 **Discuss**

Read 1 Corinthians 12:12–26. Paul describes the Church, the Christian family, as the 'Body of Christ'.

a How far do you think this could also apply to an individual Christian family?

b How much do the various members of the family need each other to enable the family to function properly?

SINGLE PARENT FAMILIES

About one in ten children are being brought up by one parent. This is usually the mother though there is an increasing number of fathers bringing up children on their own.

There are a variety of reasons for single parent families.

1 The parents have separated or divorced.

2 One of the partners has died.

3 One parent has deserted the family.

4 A girl has become pregnant and decided to keep her baby but is too young to be married.

5 The woman chooses not to marry the baby's father.

RECONSTITUTED FAMILIES

Sometimes the parent who is caring for the children gets married later. Parents who are not married when the child is born may decide to marry later, when they know each other better.

Often people who have been divorced marry again and form what is known as a 'reconstituted family'. This may result in two sets of children, a set from each marriage, becoming part of the same household. It can work out very happily. Sometimes, however, parents and children find it difficult to adapt to the new kind of relationship.

DIVORCE

People who get married do not expect to become divorced. Christians agree that marriage should be for life. They also recognize that there are difficulties in marriage which may lead to its breakdown.

When he was talking about marriage and divorce, Jesus said, 'Don't let man

In the Bible there is a book called "Hosea". It tells the story of an unhappy marriage.

Hosea married Gomer. He loved her.

But she went off with many other men...

...and left Hosea. Then she brought the children home for Hosea to look after.

But Hosea always went on loving and caring and forgiving.

"God's like this", said Hosea.

separate what God has joined together.' He also said that people should go on forgiving 'until seventy times seven'. People involved in marriage breakdown need a great deal of love, and understanding support from those around them.

CHRISTIAN VIEWPOINTS

The Eastern Orthodox Church has allowed divorce since the 11th century. There is even a very mournful service in which the marriage is ended. It is rarely used now.

Roman Catholics believe that marriage is a sacrament. This means that it is a sacred, religious act and cannot be undone. People whose marriages break down may live separately but they cannot divorce in the eyes of the Church. Even if they obtain a legal civil divorce, the Church will not recognize it. The partners cannot be remarried in church.

Catholics allow 'annulment', which is a declaration that the marriage never took place. One reason for annulment might be that one partner was mentally unstable at the time so that he or she would not have been aware that the marriage took place.

Most other Christian denominations allow divorce. Many of them think Jesus

allowed divorce after adultery, which means having a sexual relationship with someone other than the marriage partner. This was the rule in Old Testament times. Then divorce was a second best to staying married and was sometimes necessary for the protection of the wife from the anger of her husband.

REMARRIAGE

Until recently, the Church of England did not allow remarriage in church of someone who had been divorced. This rule has now changed, and bishops and parish priests are allowed to make a decision to remarry divorced people if they feel there are good reasons for doing so. Other Christian ministers have the freedom to make this decision.

CARING FOR THE CHILDREN

When marriages break down the children are likely to suffer. However carefully the parents explain what is happening, children can be confused. Many of them feel it is their fault that things have gone wrong. Sometimes they are very good at hiding their feelings. They seem to cope well and people fail to give them the support they need during the crisis. For example, they may be torn by loyalty to one parent or another, and need a great deal of understanding.

Sometimes the problems are to do with money. Courts do their best to ensure the financial support of the children, but sometimes the parent who takes on the care of the children is left with little more than state benefit. Sometimes the other partner may have to pay so much to support the children that he or she is left hardly able to cope.

CARING FOR THE PARTNERS

Each partner needs a lot of help to re-establish patterns of life. A woman who has care and control of the children and who did not work may find that she needs to get a job to help support them. Child care is very expensive. Many women do find fulfilment in a new career. Sometimes they may marry again.

It may be even more difficult for the partner who does not have care and control. They often get lonely. They want to be with their children, but are prevented from doing so. This partner can take longer to come to terms with the marriage breakup.

Divorce is not an easy solution. It leaves people facing a different set of problems.

ACTIVITIES

1 **Quick quiz**

a What percentage of children are being cared for by only one parent?

b Make a list of the reasons why some parents are looking after children on their own.

c Why do you think some parents may choose to get married after the birth of the child?

d What is a reconstituted family?

e What kind of difficulties can you think of which might occur in a reconstituted family?

f Why do you think that people who take the step of getting married rarely expect to be divorced?

g Write down one thing which Jesus said about marriage.

h What did Jesus say about forgiving people?

i Which group of Christians do not believe in divorce under any circumstances?

j What is an annulment?

k What do many other Christians believe about divorce?

l How have the Church of England's rules about remarriage changed in recent years?

m How might children feel when their parents have been divorced?

n What financial problems may there be after a divorce?

o How do some women cope with the changes that divorce makes for them?

p Why do you think that the partner who does not have care and control of the children may find life more difficult after a divorce?

MANY PRESSURES ON A MARRIAGE

2 Look at the illustration of pressures on a marriage.

a What other reasons can you think of for problems which might lead to a breakdown of marriage?

b List the pressures on marriages (including the ones you have thought of) in order of importance. There is no right answer to this. Write down what you think.

c Choose *two* of these pressures on marriage and write down what *you* think could be done to improve the situation.

housing

children

money

lack of communication

lack of appreciation

false hopes

lack of companionship

WHAT THE BIBLE TELLS US ABOUT DIVORCE

1 Look up the Bible verses in Columns A and C. Draw the chart and in Columns B and D write a sentence explaining what each verse says about divorce.

FURTHER ACTIVITIES

Ideal situation		Compromise situation	
A	B	C	D
Genesis 2:24		Deuteronomy 24:1	
Mark 10:9		Matthew 19:8	
Romans 7:2		1 Corinthians 7:12ff	
Malachi 2:16			

2 Getting help

How do you get help when you need it?

Complete the following sentences:

a If I need help in class I ....
....

b If I need help in the playground I
....

c If we breakdown when out with the car we ....

d If the washing machine breaks down we ....

e If we need some advice about our health we ....

f When we need help we usually
....

People who have family difficulties don't often ask for help until the problems have become gigantic. People who can sometimes help are called marriage guidance counsellors.

They work for an organization called Relate. There are branches of Relate in most towns. They try to help people to talk through their problems.

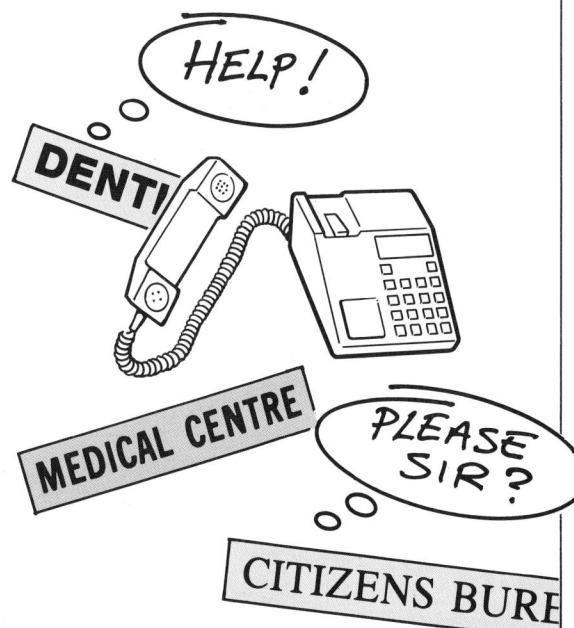

HELP!

DENTI

MEDICAL CENTRE

PLEASE SIR?

CITIZENS BURE

3 **Discuss**

a In what ways do you think it might help a family in difficulties to have the opportunity to talk about their problems with someone else?

b Can you see any difficulties in doing this?

SOME FACTS ABOUT THE DIVORCE LAWS

1857 A man could get a divorce if his wife was unfaithful
1878 A woman could separate from her husband if she could prove her husband had been cruel to her
1923 Men and women could divorce on equal terms, i.e. adultery
1937 Desertion and insanity became grounds for divorce
1969 Either partner could get a divorce for any one of these reasons:
  (i) adultery
  (ii) unreasonable behaviour
  (iii) desertion
  (iv) separation

Currently 'irretrievable breakdown of marriage' has been added.

4 **What do you think?**

a Why do you think 'unreasonable behaviour' is now the most common ground for divorce?

b Some people think that the 1969 Act has made it too easy to get a divorce. What do you think?

WHAT ADVICE WOULD YOU GIVE?

5 Read the two letters on the right carefully. Now reply to each of them. Try to give them the kind of advice which will help them to understand what the other person is feeling about the situation.

His side:
My wife recently took a job. She gets in from work at about the same time as me. Since she started work, she seems to take less trouble about making nice meals. I know I should help her in the kitchen and with some of the housework as well as looking after the children. I always feel too tired after a day at work. She seems very happy at work, and always wants to talk about it when she gets home. I've enough to cope with thinking about my own job, let alone her's as well. Do you think I ought to ask her to give up her job?

Her side:
After staying home with the children for ten years I recently went back to work. I enjoy it very much. I was rather bored at home after the children had gone to school. My husband does not seem very happy about it. He comes in from work at about the same time as me, and expects me to get the meals while he flops down in an armchair and goes to sleep. He never seems interested in my job, even though I've tried to tell him about it. It is very difficult to communicate with someone who simply goes to sleep.

Tug-of-love children sent back to Spain

M.P. IN DIVORCE SCANDAL

6 a Choose *one* of the above headlines and write the newspaper story which might be the situation behind the headline.

If you have access to a word processor and/or desk top publishing program, use it for a professional finish to your work.

b Look through the newspapers for stories which include divorced people or single parent families. Use these to help you write about the real problems which people face when they are in these situations.

WHAT DID JESUS THINK?

7 Read carefully John 8:1–11.

This story would make a good play. Begin by designing a storyboard for the action. This means drawing boxes which show the order of events and who will be on stage at any one time. This will help you to work out exactly what needs to happen to explain the story accurately.

Choose your cast and act your play.

You will now be able to answer these questions.

a Who brought the woman to Jesus?

b What were they trying to do?

c How did Jesus answer them?

d What happened next?

e Why do you think they all went away?

f What did Jesus say to the woman?

8 Discuss

Do you think that this story can help people understand more of what Jesus' attitude to divorce might have been?

9 Find out

Look in a Bible dictionary to find out about Hosea. You might like to read his story in the Book of Hosea in the Old Testament.

Hosea's marriage was full of problems. He continued loving and caring for his wife even though she went on leaving him for other men.

Hosea thought that God loved his people in the same way as Hosea loved his wife. Each of them went on caring even when the other had let them down many times.

A BIBLICAL VIEWPOINT

Money and possessions are a gift from God. They are to be regarded as 'on loan' from God, who is their real owner. Therefore, the Bible recommends, all money and possessions must be used wisely and carefully.

Read the two verses in the boxes below. They sum up the Bible's viewpoint.

> God says, 'The whole world and everything in it is mine.'
> (Psalm 50:12)

> If God gives a man wealth and property, and then lets him enjoy them, he should be grateful and enjoy what he has worked for.
> (Ecclesiastes 5:19; Luke 3:14)

The Bible also suggests that people should be satisfied with what they have. Spending all one's life trying to get more and more money, the Bible says, only leads to misery and dissatisfaction. (Ecclesiastes 5:10, 6:9; Luke 3:14)

JESUS' VIEW

Jesus pointed out that people should not measure someone's value by the number of things they own. (Luke 12:15). There are many more important things in life than money. People should resist the temptation to be greedy and selfish.

THE EARLY CHURCH

We know from the Acts of the Apostles, a book in the New Testament, that the first Christians began to share all their possessions. They tried very hard to make sure that everyone had enough food, as well as somewhere to live. People who had more than they needed were encouraged to share with the people who didn't have enough. Paul taught them that Christians should thank God

for supplying all their needs, and be generous in using their money to supply the needs of other people. They shouldn't give out of a sense of duty, though. They should give gladly and cheerfully, knowing that God was pleased with them for doing so.
(2 Corinthians 9:7ff)

CHRISTIANS NOW

Many Christians say that they believe that God will supply all their needs. This is perhaps easy to say if you live in one of the richer, northern nations. However, it is difficult to see how it works out in practice when you think about the many

1 At first...

carrots = apples = MILK

This was called "BARTER"

2 Then (about 700 BCE)...

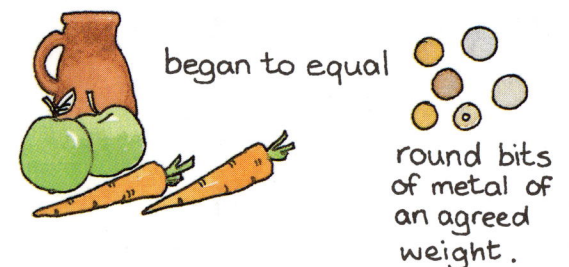

apples and carrots began to equal round bits of metal of an agreed weight.

3 Offa, King of Mercia invented the "POUND". In those days it equalled a pound weight of pure silver.

760 CE BRITAIN

4 NORMAN TIMES 1066
WILLIAM OF NORMANDY DEVALUES COINAGE BY 69%

....This didn't matter too much, as by this time coins were symbolic.

5 Henry VIII devalued it too... several times.

TUDOR TIMES 1520
HENRY DEVALUES COINAGE AGAIN!

6 Now, however, paper money is worth little in terms of paper and print, but can be said to be worth its face value because it can be exchanged for goods and services.

7 And now...

CREDIT VISA CARD

... do we need money?

Christians in parts of the world which are threatened by famine, such as Ethiopia.

Believing that God will supply all your needs is called 'living by faith'. An example of this might be someone believing it is God's will that he or she works with ex-prisoners to help them manage when they come out of prison. Their faith would be strengthened if, without asking, enough money was given to them to start this work.

ATTITUDE TO MONEY

Jesus never taught that there is anything wrong with being rich. It is only when money or possessions get in the way of having a real relationship with God that things go wrong. This was the problem with the rich young man whose story you can read in Matthew 19. His possessions mattered more to him than doing what God wanted. Similarly, in the Old Testament (Deuteronomy 8), people are warned that they are likely to forget about God when they have inherited money, and their possessions have come to them too easily.

So, Christians believe, it is our attitude to our possessions which is the difficulty. It doesn't matter what we possess, we must not let our possessions become the most important thing in our lives. People must not let their *wants* hide the fact that they have an obligation to try to meet others' *needs*.

Christians want to share things equally. However, they don't believe that people's attitudes to money can be changed by changing the structures of society. They believe that having a relationship with Jesus Christ *can* change people's attitudes both to money and to other people.

In fact, the Bible talks about 'steward-ship'. Someone who is a steward does not own resources themselves. They control resources on behalf of someone else. According to the Bible the human race is required to manage what it holds on trust from God.

ACTIVITIES

1 **Quick quiz**

a How does the Bible regard money and possessions?

b How must money be used, according to the Bible?

c What does spending all one's time trying to get more money lead to?

d What did Jesus say about money?

e In which ways did the Early Church try to share all their possessions?

f Write two sentences about Paul's attitude to money.

g Give an example of an occasion when it might be difficult to go on believing that God supplies everyone's needs.

h What do you think is the difference between wanting something and needing something?

i When might being rich make it difficult to be a Christian?

j When does the Old Testament suggest that it might be easy to forget about God?

k How do Christians believe that people's attitudes to money can be changed?

l What do you think 'stewardship' might mean?

m Write down some examples of how stewardship could apply to you.

2 Jesus reckoned it was easier to thread a needle with a camel than to get a rich man into heaven (Mark 10:25) Look up this story and then write your own saying on this subject.

DEATH OF WEALTHY BARN OWNER

THE BIGGEST BARN IN THE WORLD

NEW BARN NEVER USED

FOR SALE
DUE TO DEATH OF OWNER

3 Use Luke 12:16–21 to help you write a newspaper article reporting on the story behind this headline.

FURTHER ACTIVITIES

1 Look up the Bible verses in the chart. Use the information in them to write a paragraph with the headings shown.

Wrong attitudes to money	Right attitudes to money
Luke 12:16–21	1 Timothy 6:17
Matthew 6:31ff	Philippians 4:11–13
Luke 16:19–21	2 Corinthians 9:7f
Mark 4:15f	2 Corinthians 8:2–5

WHERE AM I?

2 Put the following people on a copy of the ladder:

Homeless person

Bank manager

Teacher

Factory worker

Victim of famine

Rich

Poor

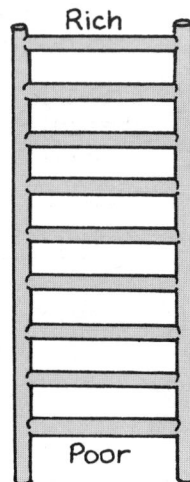

Now add yourself to the ladder, and fill in the vacant rungs with your own choice of people.

Why did you choose that rung on the ladder for yourself?

3 Read Luke 12:15.

Would Jesus have used the same method of sorting as you did? Write down some reasons for your answer.

Famous personality gives views on wealth

4 To find out what Jesus said, turn to Matthew 6:19–24.

Now write a newspaper article giving Jesus' views, as recorded in Matthew 6:19–24. Use the following headings to help you organize your article:
Money decays
Money distorts
Money divides.

Work out some examples of how these headings might be true in your own experience.

WHERE DO YOU GET YOUR MONEY?

5 Draw a chart similar to the one below which shows where you get your money from.

Type	Source
Pocket money	Mum
Presents	Relations

6 Now make a second chart which shows where adults get their money from.

HOW DO YOU SPEND IT?

7 Draw a pie chart, like the one below, which shows how you spend your weekly income.

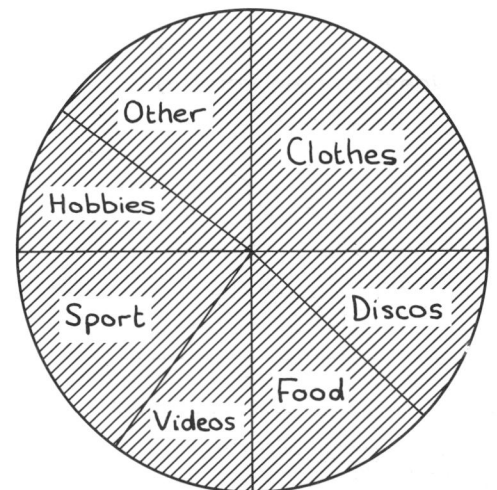

8 'Brainstorm' your group to produce a list of the things a family might need money for. You will need a big sheet of paper to write down as many ideas as possible. Don't worry about the order, just write down everything you can think of.

9 a Design a pie chart for the way you think a family might spend its money.

b Now answer these questions:
What happens if you run out of money?
What happens if a family runs out of money?
What happens if a business runs out of money?
What happens if a government runs out of money?

10 What would you do with a million pounds? Use these ideas to help you work out your answers:

a for myself

b for my family

c for others

d what else?

PRICES UP AGAIN!

Inflation now 16%

Increase in Bank Rate expected

Poor coffee crop in Brazil

Cost of new railway increased by £5 Million

PETROL PRICES UP AGAIN

COTTON CROP FAILS

Strike for more pay

11 a What do the following products cost now?

b Now use the headlines on this page to help you make a list of reasons for price increases.

c Display your information in a chart like the one shown below.

Family car

Jeans

Cornflakes

Baked beans

Coffee

Product	Reasons for increase
Cornflakes	
Beans	
Jeans	
Petrol	
Coffee	
Car	

EVERYONE WANTS TO LEARN

Small babies want to learn to crawl, then to walk, and then to progress to the next stage. People have a natural curiosity which is never totally satisfied.

LEARNING IS NATURAL

Some things are learned naturally. They are a part of growing up and living in the world. Other things are learned when someone sets out to teach us something. An example of this might be a parent telling a child a story. The child learns the story, as well as how to listen and how to join ideas together to tell a story.

CHRISTIANS IN EDUCATION

Since the Middle Ages, Christians have been involved in education. In developing countries and **missionary** situations, Christians have used education to enable people to read the Bible and understand the Christian faith as well as generally to help them. The drawings show the three main reasons why Christians are involved in education.

(i) Motivation – Christians are concerned for people

(ii) Premises – Christians have been able to use Church property to run classes of all kinds.

(iii) People – **clergy** and other church leaders have had the education themselves which enables them to pass on their skills and knowledge to others.

FORMAL LEARNING

The kind of education we receive in school includes learning things naturally, in the course of everyday living in the school community. It also includes formal education. Formal education develops our skills as well as increasing our knowledge.

Part of our education takes place at home. In the past, almost all education took place at home. In those days, people lived mostly in rural, agricultural communities. When people began to work in industry, new skills were needed. There was an increase in the knowledge available as new discoveries were made and new technologies developed. This meant that parents were no longer equipped with the appropriate knowledge to teach children everything they needed to know.

WHY ARE CHRISTIANS INTERESTED IN EDUCATION?

- Christianity began within **Judaism**. The Jews had a very strong tradition of education both at school and at home.

- Christians believe that God has given everyone certain gifts and talents. (Romans: 12, I Corinthians: 12) Education helps people to use these gifts to help other people. It helps people to develop their true potential, whatever that might be.

- Being a Christian gives people a motive for learning about the Christian faith. People need to learn to read so that they can understand the Bible. Knowing about Christianity is also vital for understanding Western culture and history.

- Christians believe that everyone is of equal importance to God. (Galatians 3:26–28) Education is one way in which Christians can help people to treat everyone equally.

- Many Christians think of teaching as a **vocation**. They see it as fulfilling the plan that they believe God has for their lives.

- Christianity is concerned with personal relationships. It does not only teach information, it teaches people how to behave towards each other. It can therefore be said to be an education for life.

- Christians believe that education should be available to everyone. Everyone has unique talents which are given them by God, and should therefore be given the chance to develop these talents. Christians recognize that success in education should never be measured only in terms of academic achievement. Instead they say that everyone has a gift which can enrich the world. To be educated is to have learned how to use that gift in the service of others.

NOTES/DATABASE

Look up the following words in the glossary. Then use the definitions to make suitable entries for your notebook or database.

Missionary	Judaism
Clergy	Vocation

EDUCATION IN BIBLICAL TIMES

In early Old Testament times, children learned skills from their mothers and fathers. There was no 'school' for ordinary children. Religious knowledge, about the Jewish religious rules and about festivals, was passed on at home. Boys were expected to follow the same trade as their fathers.

Jewish education in New Testament times was divided into three sections:

1 Academic

By the time of Jesus, boys went to a synagogue school from the age of six. Girls were still educated by their mothers. At school, boys learned to read Hebrew, which was regarded as a tool to help them with other subjects like geography, history, law and literature. These four subjects were learned from the 39 books of the Old Testament.

Bright boys were sent to Jerusalem to 'sit at the feet of a rabbi'. That meant literally sitting, listening and absorbing the rabbi's teachings. It was therefore unusual when Jesus, aged 12, was said to be 'both hearing them and asking them questions'. Some Jewish boys, like Paul of Tarsus, studied at a university.

2 Vocational

Every boy was expected to learn a trade. This was a way of making sure that everyone could do something to contribute to society in a practical way. Paul, for example, a university graduate, was also trained as a tentmaker. He often had to earn his living by using his trade.

3 Religious

Children learned about their religion at home. They needed to know the part they would have to play in the religious festivals which were held in the home.

A Religious learning was a part of education for Jews in the Old Testament and is still important today

1 Quick quiz

a Give an example of natural learning.

b What is formal learning?

c Why were more schools needed when people began to work in industry?

d What are the three reasons why Christians are able to be involved in education?

e Write down some of the reasons why Christians wish to be involved in education.

f What do Christians mean by *vocation*?

g How do Christians think that success in education should be measured?

2 Now answer these questions:

a How did children receive their education in Old Testament times?

b How were girls educated in the time of Jesus?

c At what age did Jewish boys go to school?

d What subjects did they learn?

e What were the three main divisions of Jewish education?

f Do you think it was a good idea to make every boy learn a trade? Give some reasons for your answer.

FULSTON MANOR
TIMETABLE 1989–1990

Name Katherine Hughes   Set 1

Day	1	2	3	4	5
Monday	I.T. RM 27 →	R.E. RM 5.	HISTORY RM 6.		
Tuesday	SCIENCE RM 26 →	FRENCH RM 15.	GEOG. RM		
Wednesday	ENG. RM 9.	C.D.T. → RM 22 →			

3 Look at your own school timetable. Decide which subjects fit in with each of the divisions of Jewish education. Now draw up a new timetable form. Use three different colours for academic, vocational and religious to show on your timetable which of your subjects belongs in each category.

Is there any way in which your subjects do *not* fit in with this division?

Do you think your education would be more relevant to the rest of your life if it fitted in more closely with the three Jewish divisions? Give reasons for your answers.

1 Here are some topics for you to discuss in groups:

How big should a school be?

Should everyone have an identical education?

What kind of test should there be?

Should schools be more a real part of the community?

Should schools train pupils to do specific jobs?

Do schools really prepare pupils for life?

What should be learned in a school?

2 In a group discuss and then draw up your own school timetable. You should include all areas which will be of use in the *whole* of life. You need not stick to the same subject names as the ones you have in your school, or to the same times or number of lessons that you have now.

FURTHER ACTIVITIES

3 **Brainstorm session**

What advantages and disadvantages can you see in everyone being expected to learn the same things?

Use a large sheet of paper or flip chart and a marker pen to collect everyone's ideas in a two-column chart.

WHERE IN THE WORLD?

4 a Look at the pictures of the schools. Locate each one on the map of the world.

b Which ones are in
(i) the rich North
(ii) the poor South?

c What similarities are there between the pictures of schools in the North?

d What similarities are there between pictures of schools in the South?

e How do you feel about the North/South differences?

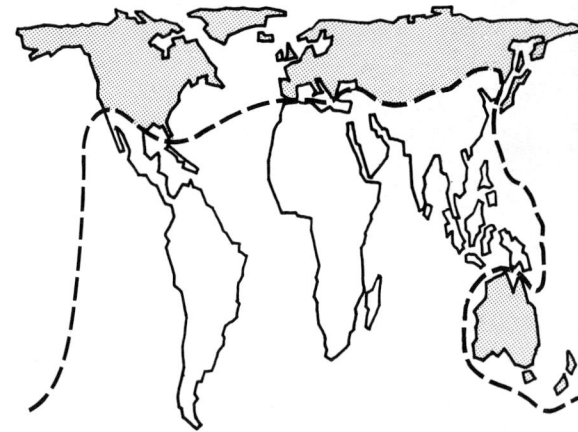

B A science lesson in the UK

C A homeland school in South Africa

5 Imagine you are members of your school Finance Committee. A rich benefactor has left you the sum of £25,000 and you have to decide how to spend it.

a How would you spend the money in a way which would benefit the pupils of your school?

b Discuss your ideas in groups.

D Media Studies in the UK

E Two classes in one classroom in Bolivia

TWIN SCHOOLS

6 Some schools in richer nations are twinned with schools in poorer countries.

a Do you think this is a good idea? Explain the reasons for your answer.

b Copy and complete the following chart:

Ways in which it could benefit Third World School	Ways in which it could benefit school in richer nation

REACH OUT VILLAGE MINISTRY

On the shores of Lake Victoria in Uganda there is a Christian orphanage and school run by Danial Nkata. A group of Christians in Kent have been collecting sewing machines to send to this school. These have been used to make clothes for the children and to begin a village industry which will help the whole community.

There is no free education in Uganda, and people go to incredible lengths to pay their school fees. The people of this little village are extremely poor but they sacrifice food and clothing for themselves in order to send their children to school. The reason is that there is 50 per cent unemployment in Uganda and the children will have some chance, however small, of a job if they can read, write and speak English.

Dorothy, from Campala, sits each day in the market selling plastic plates in order to send her children to school. Her husband has left her. He sends enough money to the family for food, but not enough to pay school fees. Dorothy came to England with her church choir. She found it difficult to understand English parents who were not keen to make the most of the opportunity of free education which children have in the UK. In Uganda, all books and equipment have to be paid for by the parents. A child who does not work hard is asked to leave so that someone who will work can have the school place instead.

ONE WAY TO HELP

Joan, a Christian from Britain, went on holiday to India. In her hotel she became friendly with her servant. She wanted to help him, and so asked him what he would like her to do for him. He said, 'pay some money for my children to go to school'. Joan arranged to send a monthly cheque to cover the school fees for his two children, and now receives regular reports on their progress. This is Joan's way of thanking God for her own prosperity.

7 **Discuss**

Why do you think that people in the poorer countries are prepared to make sacrifices to pay for their children's education?

THE BIBLICAL VIEWPOINT

In the Bible, God is seen as a worker. Jesus said, 'My father always works, and so do I.' (John 5:17) In working even on the **sabbath**, when Jewish law forbade work, Jesus claimed to be imitating God, his father.

In the Old Testament, God was seen as a workman. He is described as a potter, busy with moulding clay in the work of **creation**.

Jesus, it seems, followed in Joseph's footsteps and worked as a carpenter in Nazareth. Paul points proudly to his own work as a tentmaker to show that he has never cost Christians money for his keep.

A Some people work alone . . .

Work is seen as a social necessity. Every group of people has needed to work to be able to feed, clothe and house itself. In different countries and different times, the way in which the work has been shared out has varied. Christianity expects work to be done for the benefit of others, and to contribute to the common good.

According to the Bible, people are expected to manage the earth's resources, to do creative work, to use their gifts and talents properly, and to accept God's 'vocation' or plan for their lives.

One of the ways in which the Bible refers to Christians is as a 'body'. (Romans:12, 1 Corinthians:12) Every part of the body is as useful as every other part. This means that Christians don't see one job as being more important than any other job. Paul pointed out that the most useful jobs are often the ones we try to ignore. (1 Corinthians 12:22) This means that all jobs which are done for the common good are of equal importance. The factory worker has a vocation to a job just as much as a priest or bishop.

B . . . others work for very large companies

NATURAL ACTIVITY

Work is a natural activity. People need to work to stay alive. (Genesis 2:15) Through working, people can share in God's creative activity. (Genesis 1:28) Although work can sometimes lead to boredom, or even pain, it is also healthy. It often brings spiritual well being. Even being tired at the end of a good day's work can bring its own sense of satisfaction. Work is a way of obtaining the things we need to go on living, such as food, shelter and clothes, and is at the same time a way of enriching our lives with beauty and enjoyment.

WORK IS NOT THE SAME AS PAID EMPLOYMENT

Paid employment is one way in which some work can be organized. There are many kinds of work which people do which are not paid employment, for example, housework. In some countries, particularly in rural communities, paid employment is unusual. In industrialized countries, paid employment is the more usual way of organizing much of the common work.

WORKING HARD

Some people in paid employment work harder than others. They might work hard so that they will earn more money. People will usually work better if they have a good employer.

Employers have a responsibility towards the people who work for them, as well as towards their customers and the owners of the company. Christians think there is something wrong with a company which is only run for profit and does not have consideration for the people who work in it.

Christians at work should accept the need to work as well for a bad employer as for a good one. However, they should also stand up for what is right and persevere to make conditions better for the workforce.

A Christian called Dr Wilfred Grenfell was a missionary among the Inuit, or Eskimos. He once said, 'Being a Christian is doing something, anything, well.'

What does *vocation* mean? *Vocation* means 'calling'. It is the instinctive feeling that some job of work is exactly right for *you*.

Look up Proverbs 6:6
Did you know that you can learn a lesson about work from *ants*?

NOTES/DATABASE

Look up the following words in the glossary. Then use the definitions to make suitable entries for your notebook or database.

Sabbath   Creation

KEY IDEAS ABOUT WORK IN THE BIBLE

2 Look up the following verses to find some important ideas about work:

Matthew 25:14–29	Work is what God expects people to do
Matthew 25:31–45	Work is a Christian duty
Luke 12:13–21	Working for the wrong reasons
Colossians 3:23f	Reasons for a Christian to work
Acts 18:1–4	Paul's ideas about work
2 Thessalonians 3:7–12 Proverbs 6:6–11 Proverbs 26:13–16	Being lazy

ACTIVITIES

1 **Quick quiz**

a What is one way in which God is seen in the Bible?

b What did Jesus claim to be doing when he was once accused of working on the sabbath?

c What job did Jesus probably do?

d How did Paul earn his living?

e Why does every group of people need to work?

f Why do Christians expect to work?

g What are four of the reasons the Bible gives for working?

h Why do you think that Christians do not see one job as being more important than another?

i Explain the difference between work and paid employment.

j What responsibilities do you think an employer might need to have towards the workforce?

k What reasons might a Christian have for trying to obtain improved conditions for the workforce?

C God says 'Look after the world'

UN Declaration of Human Rights

'Everyone has the right to work, to free choice of employment, to just and favourable conditions of work, and to protection against unemployment.'

FURTHER ACTIVITIES

1 On the diagram you can see the advantages and disadvantages of a multinational company and the advantages of a local company. What could be the *disadvantages* of the local company?

"We could move to another country"

cash flow   taxes   new laws   staffing problems

SUNRISE BREAD COMPANY

BOOTHS
HOME-MADE BREAD
FRESH EVERY DAY

SUNRISE

SUNRISE NATIONWIDE 7 DAY DELIVERY

profits may go abroad

loyal to smaller local area

employing local people

move to somewhere where the wages are lower

redundancies

move to where workers are not so well protected

WHERE SHALL WE MAKE IT?

2 What kinds of product can be manufactured in a centralized factory and distributed all over the world? What needs to be made locally?

Copy and complete the chart on the right:

Centrally made	Locally made
Cars	Cakes

MARTHA AND MARY

3 Read the story of Martha and Mary in Luke 10:30f.

Martha was told off by Jesus for letting her work get too important.

Mary was praised for being herself.

a What do you think about the behaviour of the two sisters?

b Why do you think Jesus took this attitude?

Relax!

I haven't had a day off in weeks.

4 Look up the following verses. These tell you more about Jesus' attitude to work.
Matthew 6:26–29. The birds and the flowers are blessed by God without having to work.
John 13:1–17
Mark 10:42f
Matthew 25:31–46

Jesus saw work as service to others.

Now write about Jesus' attitude to work.

5 Look up the following verses. Draw the chart and then enter the verses in the appropriate column of the chart.

2 Thessalonians 3:6–11
Colossians 3:23
Ephesians 6:5–7
Proverbs 19:15, 6:6–11, 26:14–16
Psalms 104:19, 23
Genesis 3:17–19
Deuteronomy 24:14f
Jeremiah 22:13

Interesting work	Tedious work

6 What work would *you* find interesting and what would you find tedious?

Draw a chart like the one above putting what you find interesting and tedious in the appropriate columns.

JOB-SHARING

7 Job-sharing schemes are ones in which one job is divided between two people.

a Make a list of jobs which might be suitable for this scheme.

b What kinds of people might benefit from a scheme of this kind? Give reasons for your choices.

Survey

Do you enjoy your job? Yes/No

Would you retire early if you had the chance? Yes/No

How do you spend your spare time? _____

_____

_____

Is work the same as paid employment? Yes/No

What other jobs have you done? _____

8 Ask some adults from a variety of different occupations and age groups the questions in the survey above. Use bar charts to help you display your information clearly. If you have a suitable computer program this might be helpful. The form could be produced using a desk top publishing program, and you could display the statistics using a business graphics program.

9 Think about the instructions, and the temptations to ignore them, in the chart. How would you apply each of these instructions and how could you overcome the temptations:
a at school
b at work?

No skiving	I'm far too tired for work
Be on time	It's already too late.
Be honest — They won't miss just a little stationery	Attend regularly — I'd rather go fishing today.

HOW WE USED TO LIVE

10 Interview some elderly people about working conditions in the past. How do they think things have changed? You may find that it is better to record this on audio or video tape.

Here is Jean O'Hara's account of working in a mill. She was born in 1906.

'I had to leave school and start work when I was 13 because there were eight more brothers and sisters after me. I started work at 6 am and worked a 12-hour day. The mills in Lancashire were the only thing an ordinary girl could do if she didn't want to go into service. In the mill it was hard work, and the air was very thick. It was sometimes hard to breathe. I got five shillings a week, and had to give my mother four shillings of it. It was a penny each day for my tram fare, so I'd walk to the mill when I could.'

Ted, also born in 1906, was chosen to go to a grammar school, and then got a scholarship to an art college. However, his parents could not afford to let him go to college so he ran away to sea as a galley boy. In those days you could still work your way up in the Merchant Navy, and he ended up as a captain. Later, he served in the Royal Navy during World War 2, commanding a landing ship. The final years of his career were as a teacher on the Training Ship *Arethusa*.

D Inside a Lancashire mill

E A school ship – the *TS Arethusa*

WORK IS NOT THE SAME AS PAID EMPLOYMENT

Work should not be confused with paid **employment**. We fill our time in order to keep ourselves and others alive. This activity is also a way of fulfilling our purpose in the world. We are not always paid for the work we do. Many 'unemployed' people in fact work very hard.

AGRICULTURAL COMMUNITIES

All communities share out the work of the **community**. The word 'unemployment' might not make sense in a simple agricultural community. Each member does the job they are old enough and capable enough to do without supervision. They learn other tasks from people who are more experienced. Finally everyone shares in food, clothing and shelter.

INDUSTRIALIZED SOCIETIES

Industrialized countries, like the UK and most of Europe, have more complicated systems of organizing their work. The community still has tasks to do to produce food, clothing and shelter, but jobs are shared differently. One person may do a job which earns money so that he or she can purchase these necessities.

Some of the work of an industrialized society is done by people who are in paid employment. Much of the work is done within family situations, and some work is done by **volunteers**. People who are not in paid employment do a great deal of the work of society, both within their own families and as volunteers in the community.

REASONS FOR UNEMPLOYMENT

People become unemployed for a variety of reasons. A woman, for example, might give up paid employment because she is going to have a baby. She will not be counted in the unemployment figures because she is not looking for work, and not usually receiving unemployment benefit.

Sometimes a person may have taken a temporary job like fruit picking or working in the leisure industry, and becomes unemployed at the end of the season.

All too often, especially when interest rates are high, companies who manufacture goods need to cut costs. Their goods may not be selling because many people are unemployed and cannot afford to buy things. The company will then need to lay off workers.

There are also times when a company becomes bankrupt, stops trading and lays off its workers.

A Unemployed Christians can use their talents to help the community . . .

B . . . in many different ways

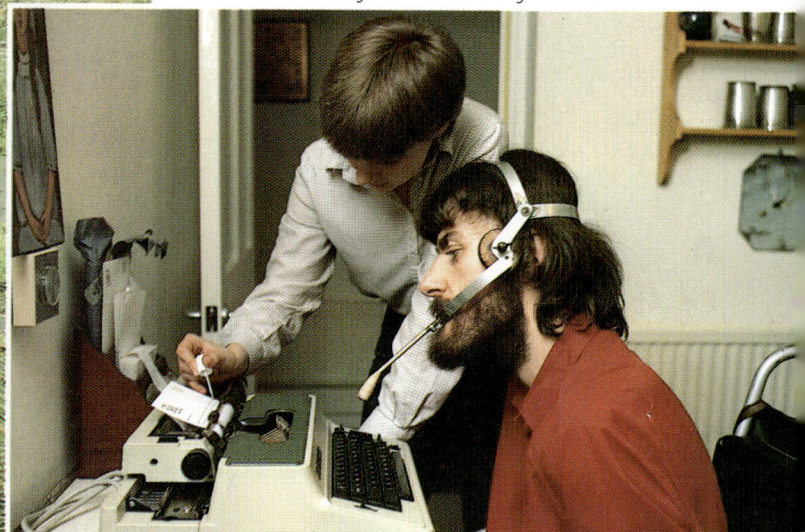

THE EFFECTS OF UNEMPLOYMENT

When someone is unemployed, they often become depressed. Sometimes, they have a feeling of being useless and unwanted. This is because society tends to measure a person's worth by the job they do.

Older people often feel that they will never get another job. Sometimes they call this 'being left on the scrap heap'.

Younger people who have never had a job often begin to feel desperate. They feel that they will be looking for a job for ever. They resent having less money than their friends who have jobs.

It is the younger and the older members of society who are more likely to be unemployed for long periods of time. Statistics show that middle-aged people who are unemployed get another job fairly soon.

THE BIBLE'S VIEW OF UNEMPLOYMENT

Jesus would never have measured someone's worth by the job they do. He valued everyone equally, whatever their position in society.

St Paul valued all people for their unique contribution to society. When he says that the person who won't work should not be allowed to eat, he is not referring to people who have become unemployed through no fault of their own. He is referring to people who refuse to work.

A POSITIVE VIEW

Christians believe that God has a special plan for everyone's life. This includes the job which they do. After all, they believe that he has given them the unique gifts needed to do their job.

God's plan also includes periods of unemployment. Christians believe that these are just as much a part of God's vocation for their lives as the periods of paid employment.

If Christians become unemployed they should use the time both to work for the good of the community and to think through God's purpose for their life. This might mean the individual needs to say, 'Is this job really what God wants me to do with my life?' 'Should I begin to think about God's purpose for the rest of my life?'

This process has led many Christians to change their lifestyle. One shop owner became a teacher. A teacher became a prison chaplain, while another very senior teacher gave up her job to work as a volunteer with homeless men.

Whether they are in paid employment or not, Christians believe that God's plan for their lives is a perfect one. Unemployment, seen positively, can help people to fulfil God's vocation for their lives.

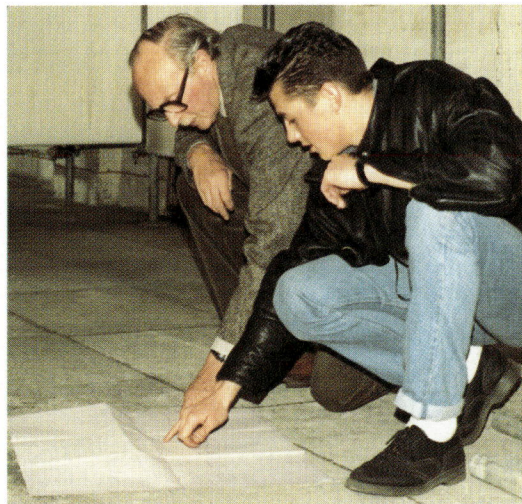

C and D The CATHEX project in Rochester and Canterbury Cathedral: the Church can help in training people

ACTIVITIES

1 **Quick quiz**

a Why is it important not to confuse work with paid employment?

b How do agricultural communities share out the work of the community?

c In what ways is the work shared out in an industrialized society?

d What kinds of work do people who are not in paid employment do?

e Make a list of the reasons why someone might become unemployed?

f Why do you think someone who is unemployed might become depressed?

g Why do you think it is the younger and older members of the workforce who are the most likely to become unemployed?

h What do you think Paul meant when he said that the person who would not work should not eat?

i What do Christians believe about unemployment?

j What might a Christian think about during a period of unemployment?

FURTHER ACTIVITIES

1 If you left school without being able to get a job, which would you do:

a work experience

b more education

c use existing skills to start your own business

d keep trying to get a job

e community service?

Write down some reasons for your answer.

E Getting a job is harder for some people: who do you think might face difficulties?

HOW WOULD YOU COPE?

2 At school you have been used to a timetable. Bells, buzzers or pips have organized your day. Work out a timetable for how you would organize your week if you were unemployed. Remember that on one day in a fortnight you will need to sign on. (This means entering your name on the list of unemployed people every fortnight so that you will receive some money for your basic needs.)

APRIL

SUNDAY 1ST	8 a.m. Church 10 am. Football
MONDAY 2ND	9 a.m. Listen to 'Jobline' 10 a.m. Go to Job centre
TUESDAY 3RD	9 a.m. Listen to 'Jobline' 10 a.m. Go to Job Club 2 p.m. Help at old peoples' club
WEDNESDAY 4TH	

APRIL

THURSDAY 5TH	2 p.m. Sign on Get local paper Read jobs column
FRIDAY 6TH	Help at Youth Club.
SATURDAY 7TH	SHOPPING Go swimming
NOTES	

Dear Auntie,

My son is unemployed. He did not work at school, and although we paid for him to go to college, we soon found that he was not attending. We have tried to persuade him to get a job, but he only seems willing to stay in bed all day. As I work very hard, I resent going out to work in the morning leaving a son of eighteen snoring away in bed. He contributes nothing to the household, and although he gets some unemployment benefit, he is always short of money. How can I persuade him to get a job? He won't write off for any of the jobs in the paper, and laughs if I mention the job centre.

Britain's no-hope children

By ROGER TODD

BRITAIN'S school leavers have never had it so bad, according to a survey out today.

The thousands who can't get a job have become the lost generation with little hope for the future.

They are left destitute if their parents won't keep them.

The survey, by the Family Policy Studies Centre, says youngsters can't get social security until they are 18.

And even then it is at a reduced rate.

Centre director Malcolm Wicks said: "Wages for those who manage to get a job have been cut.

"Many training schemes are low-paid and inadequate."

The survey found that teenagers whose fathers were on the dole were twice as likely to end up jobless.

One in seven who qualify for university were forced to look for work instead because of parental pressure to earn money.

F Young people may find it difficult to find their first job

500 steel jobs axed

MORE than 500 jobs will be axed when two steel plants are closed, it was announced yesterday.

Industrial conglomerate Trafalgar House is shutting down structural steel works at Cambuslang, near Glasgow, and Trafford Park, Manchester, to concentrate production on its modern factory at Darlington.

The Glasgow plant has 319 staff and Manchester employs 230. The closures will be phased in over four months.

Workers have been told that where possible they will be transferred to other plants.

3 How would you reply to this letter? Think carefully about the advice you would give. It is not an easy problem to solve.

G Many people lose their jobs when industries, like this colliery, close down

4 Look carefully at the newspaper articles about unemployment, as well as the other information in this unit.

Imagine that you are a team of television journalists preparing an in-depth report about unemployment. Use the articles and the rest of the information in this unit to help you prepare your report. You will need to prepare outline scripts for this programme. It may be possible for you to visit a 'Job Club' and ask the members if you might interview them. You can find out about Job Clubs at the Job Centre. The staff there may be able to give you useful information about the kinds of vacancies available in your area.

You should also find out about any schemes for the unemployed in your area. These will include national schemes like Job Start and Employment Training, as well as local schemes which are often run by Christian churches.

If you have 'on-line' facilities, linking your school computer with other schools, it may be possible for you to collect information from another area as well. If you live in a rural area, try to collect information from an urban area. If you live in the north, try to collect information from the south and vice versa.

5 **Discuss**

How should Christians be responding to job losses? In which ways can Christians look at these problems positively?

GOD IS INTERESTED IN LEISURE

Christians believe that the work they do is part of God's plan for their lives. This must mean that God is equally interested in leisure.

WHAT IS LEISURE?

Leisure is quite difficult to define. What is a leisure-time activity for one person is often work for another. For example, someone may be very interested in old cars, and spend all their leisure time restoring them. Someone else may in fact work in a garage which specializes in such restoration work. Sometimes a person spends leisure time doing similar things to those which he or she may do at work. An example of this might be a chef who enjoys making meals for friends.

A One person's hobby may be another person's job

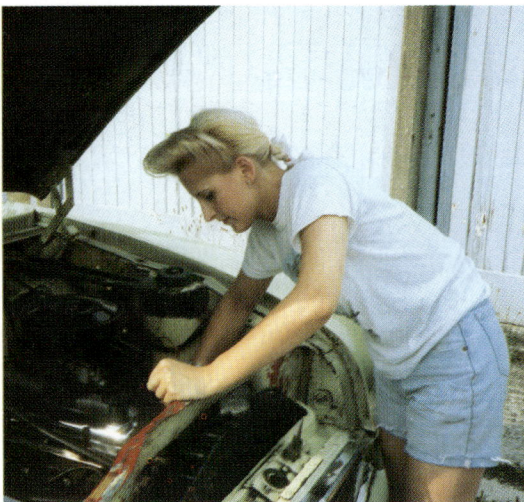

LEISURE MEANS CHOICE

Leisure allows us to choose what we want to do. PE may be a good lesson at school, and you may choose to swim with a club at weekends. This kind of leisure-time activity can often be more strenuous than the work which we do.

RELAXING IS IMPORTANT

Leisure also contains an element of relaxation. A reasonable leisure-time pursuit is sitting down in front of the television with your feet up.

HELPING OTHERS

Some people like to use spare time to help others. It is difficult to call this kind of **voluntary work** 'leisure'. It is a chance to help other people, and the

B Using leisure time to help other people

C An active use of leisure time

change from usual activity does provide a kind of relaxation as well as the opportunity to meet other people.

DON'T WORK ALL THE TIME

Some Christians want to give the impression that it is right to go on working as much as possible. This is especially true of jobs like being a doctor or a vicar. Some vicars boast that they can't remember when they had a day off. However, everyone needs rest and relaxation, as well as a time doing things with their families or friends which are different from their usual activities. Even God rested on the seventh day.

BIBLICAL ATTITUDE

The idea of a regular day off per week came from the Jews. The Old Testament commanded Jews to take a regular day off per week. It was a day of complete rest and relaxation for everyone – no working yourself, and no making other people work. Even animals were given a day off. Women didn't do any cooking, and no one went on journeys.

This day off was intended as a time of 're-creation'. According to the story in Genesis, the seventh day was the day on which God rested after he had created the world. He looked back at his work in the previous six days and saw it was good. The sabbath became the Jewish opportunity to do exactly the same thing – to look back over the previous week's work and to be satisfied with it. It also became a time for Jewish people to think about God's goodness to them.

DIFFERENCES IN ATTITUDE

To someone in paid employment leisure seems very precious. It is a luxury which needs careful planning to achieve real re-creation.

To someone who is unemployed, there may be difficulties in planning leisure time. It is not easy to use leisure creatively, especially if you have too much time on your hands.

The result of too much leisure is often surplus energy with no real outlet for it. This results in boredom. Trouble sometimes follows such as vandalism, destruction of property and violence to other people, including a person's own family. Sometimes drug abuse and alcoholism are the direct result of this kind of boredom. However, too much leisure can also be used positively. Christians see unemployment as giving them the freedom to do what God wants them to do at that moment. This points the way to an alternative for people who are unemployed. They have the freedom to ask, 'Where can I make my best contribution to the community?'

NOTES/DATABASE

Look up the following words in the glossary. Then use the definitions to make suitable entries for your notebook or database.

Leisure   Voluntary work

ACTIVITIES

1 Quick quiz

a What do Christians call God's plan for their lives?

b Why do they think God is just as interested in leisure?

c Why do you think it is hard to define leisure?

d Write down some examples of how someone might choose to spend their leisure time in activities which are similar to those things they do at work.

e How can leisure be more strenuous than work?

f Why do you think relaxation is important?

g How can people use their leisure time to help others?

h Why do you think some people feel proud of never having a day off?

i Why is this not a sensible attitude?

j What was the sabbath like for the Jews?

k Why do you think many Jews stick to this idea of the sabbath now?

l How does the story in Genesis help us to understand more about leisure?

m What problems can you see if someone has too much leisure?

n How can the leisure resulting from unemployment be used positively?

D The Tall Ships Race: many people enjoy competing or watching

'You have six days in which to do your work, but the seventh day is a day of rest dedicated to God. On that day, no one is to do any work.'
(Exodus 10:9)

'There were so many people coming and going that Jesus and his disciples didn't even have time to eat. So he said to them "Let us go off to some place where we will be alone and you can rest for a while."'
(Mark 6:31:f)

2 Discuss

Read the two quotations from the Bible carefully. How do these two quotations help us to understand the need for leisure?

45

FURTHER ACTIVITIES

Survey

1 **How do you spend your leisure time?**
How much time in a week do you spend on the following activities?

Activity	Time spent
Sport	_____
Television/Videos	_____
Music	_____
Hobbies	_____
Clubs	_____
Reading	_____
Helping at home	_____
Helping others	_____
Worshipping God	_____

Ask every member of the class to bring in something which shows their leisure-time activities. This could be used for a display.

2 Make a bar chart showing your own leisure-time activity pattern.

3 Plan a speech about what you do in your spare time. If you do something rather unusual, make sure you describe it clearly. Other people may be interested enough to want to do the same thing.

4 You choose some of your leisure-time activities, whereas some of the things you do in your spare time are imposed on you. Copy and complete the following chart showing which things you have chosen to do, and which things you are *made* to do.

Voluntary activities	Things I have to do
Swimming	Tidying my room

5 In the UK people generally spend about one-third of their money on leisure. Divide your money up and see if it fits into that pattern.

Necessities	Leisure
New socks	Audio Tape

6 **Discuss in groups**

How might Christians want to spend some of their leisure time?

7 Local leisure database

If you have access to a suitable computer program, create a database of all the leisure-time activities which are available in your area. Many of the churches provide some of the activities. Make sure you include these.

E Churches may organize trips to leisure centres

8 Leisure should be balanced

Copy and complete the following chart.

What did you do in the last week?	
On your own	
With friends	
With family	

9 Now draw a pie chart of how your time was divided.

LEISURE INDUSTRY

10 A whole industry has grown up around leisure.

Find out what jobs there are in the leisure industry. It might be helpful to group them under the following headings:

- Sport, Health and Fitness
- Travel and Tourism
- Catering and Accommodation

It might be helpful to keep the information about each of these jobs on a database of Leisure Industry Employment. This could be useful in the Careers Department of your school.

VENTURE CLUB

THE HAVEN VENTURE CLUB AT BONIFORD, DUPORTH, BRIDFORD BAY, AND THORNESS BAY

Welcome to a holiday club with a difference!

The Venture Club takes place at four of our top parks during the school holidays and it's every child's guarantee of the most exciting holiday experience of a lifetime.

They'll be supervised by our specially selected Haven Venture Club Instructors who'll provide youngsters aged between 8 to 15 the opportunity to have a go at a whole host of all action sports and activities.

Events like abseiling, expeditions, archery, fencing, tennis, netball, cricket, rounders, orienteering, assault course, fitness tests and swimming (with lessons).

There's plenty of time too for participants to follow the activities of their choice, outside of the organised programme of events. And the week ends with a terrific farewell Barbecue!

THE HAVEN VENTURE CLUB HOW TO JOIN

There's a charge of £16 per child for a full week and the Venture Club is available at the parks concerned during the week commencing 26th May and then between 14th July to 1st September inclusive. Full details of the Venture Club and a Booking Form will be sent to you with your holiday booking confirmation. Please apply direct to the Park for booking of this special facility. Numbers are limited, so please book early.

WHAT'S NEW WHAT'S NEW

Our continued investment and expansion means we are able to offer even more new facilities again this year!

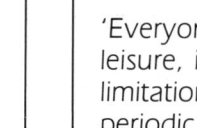
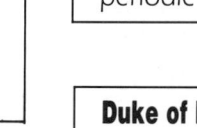
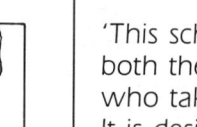
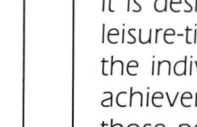
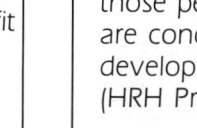
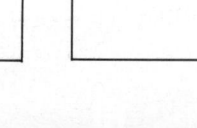

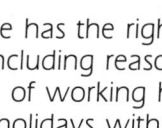
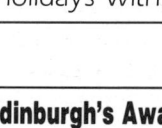
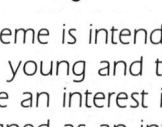
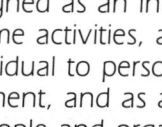
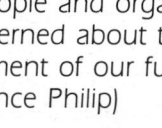
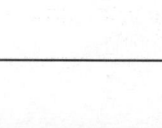

WEST BAY
New family sized Park for 1990

BEACON FELL VIEW
New small and friendly Park for 1990

SHEERNESS
New small and friendly Park for 1990

PRESTHAVEN
Refurbished Sands Night Spot
Refurbished Indoor Fun Pool

BRYNOWEN
New Indoor Pool

WHITBY
Extended Club Room

BLUE DOLPHIN
New Adventure Playground

PRIMROSE VALLEY
Refurbished Indoor Fun Pool
Pitch & Putt

REIGHTON SANDS
New Indoor Pool
New Adventure Playground

GOLDEN SANDS
New Indoor Fun Palace
New Adventure Playground

COMBE HAVEN
New Conqueror Centre
with Food Court
Extended Club
Upgraded Precinct

THORNESS BAY
Venture Club
Extended Club Room

LITTLESEA
New Indoor Pool

DUPORTH
Luxury 3 & 4 bedroom
self-catering chalets

BONIFORD
New Indoor Fun Palace

STARBURST WEEKENDS
New for 1990 – our great Starburst Weekends, with top quality entertainment from Friday night until Sunday lunchtime.

Choose from
* Starburst Country and Western Weekend at Combe Haven. 18th–20th May.
* Starburst Nostalgia Weekend at Devon Cliffs. 27th–29th April.
* Starburst Sounds of the Big Bands Weekend at Primrose Valley. 27th–29th April.

See page 95 for details.

---

11 Choices

Christianity involves choosing leisure pursuits which are in line with Christian teaching. What kind of choices do you think a Christian might need to make about what they do in their leisure time?

It has been predicted that leisure time will increase in the next few years. This will widen our choices. How do you think this may change the way we choose to use our leisure time?

UN Declaration on Human Rights

'Everyone has the right to rest and leisure, including reasonable limitation of working hours and periodic holidays with pay.'

12 Imagine this is a headline in your local paper.

Plan how to spend money on a new leisure scheme in your own area. It may use land which is derelict at the moment. It may be a new sports complex. It might use a stretch of river or canal which has not been developed, or it might be a scheme to attract tourists to your area.

New Leisure Scheme for Area

Discuss
a What the needs are.
b How many jobs it might create.

Draw sets of plans for the scheme, and work out how it will be of benefit to people in your area.
Leisure for some creates work for others. Why is this?

Duke of Edinburgh's Award Scheme

'This scheme is intended to help both the young and those people who take an interest in their welfare. It is designed as an introduction to leisure-time activities, a challenge to the individual to personal achievement, and as a guide to those people and organizations who are concerned about the development of our future citizens.'
(HRH Prince Philip)

UN Declaration on Human Rights

'Everyone has the right to a standard of living adequate for the health and security of their family, including . . . a home.'

A SHARED ROOF

Christians have always wanted to share their homes with others. In Acts 2 and Acts 4, the early Christians in Jerusalem shared their possessions and their homes. They had meals in each other's houses, and shared all their possessions. Some of them, who had extra property which they did not need, such as a house or field, sold these so that there was more money to share between members of the Christian community.

Christians began to worship in homes. Only later did they begin to build special places for worship. The Christian home is still the centre of Christian life and worship. Many Christians believe it is part of their responsibility to God to share their homes with others.

A You may live in a rented house . . .

OWNING YOUR OWN HOME

A house is probably the most expensive thing any of us will ever buy. At present in the UK they cost around five or six times someone's annual salary. Building societies will lend about 2½–3 times someone's annual salary. There are therefore problems facing people buying a house. If they are a couple, for example, both partners may need to work. They will face the decision of either having no children, or leaving it until later before they start a family.

B . . . or own your own home . . .

RENTED ACCOMMODATION

Although some rented accommodation can be good, it is generally expensive. Properties with reasonable rents are often of a poorer quality. There are usually long waiting lists for council housing. Much of the good council housing has now been bought by the tenants. This means that very often, people who live in council owned property live in the houses which no one wanted to buy. There are two main reasons for this:
a It is poor quality
b It is in an unpopular area.

People who live in good rented accommodation often have to pay as much for it as if they were buying their own houses. They are therefore unable to save enough money for the deposit on a house of their own.

There are two main ways in which rented accommodation can be improved.

a Sometimes a local authority undertakes a slum clearance programme. This means they knock down old houses so that new homes can be built. Often

C . . . . or be one of the many people on a Council waiting list

the new houses are a long way from the ones which were demolished, so communities are split up and people moved away from their friends. When this happens, it takes a long time for a community to be re-established. People take time to make new friends and to turn their new houses into homes where they feel secure. If the new houses are high-rise developments there can also be many problems of loneliness especially for old people and for families with young children.

b A more popular solution now is to restore older houses. This can sometimes be done without disrupting the community too much. Housing associations are organizations which are often involved in this kind of restoration work. The Quakers have been particularly keen on encouraging their members to be involved in housing associations. They have also built houses on church land, and rented them at reasonable rents.

Some housing associations provide for one particular group of people. For example, Car-Gomm Houses, a Christian group, provide accommodation for single men.

In Kent there is a group called ACORN. This is providing sheltered accommodation for young adults who are both physically and mentally disabled. Their parents grouped together to organize the raising of money to provide somewhere for these young people to live with dignity when they left school.

HOSTELS

Hostels provide temporary accommodation for people with immediate housing problems. Christian organizations such as the Salvation Army, the Shaftesbury Homes, and the Church Army have been very active in providing hostels for groups of people such as battered wives, homeless teenagers and adults, as well as ex-offenders.

SQUATS

A squat is either land or property which was empty and which has been taken over by a group of people. There is often no water, no power and no sanitation. There are two main reasons why people live in squats.

a Some people are protesting against the rich people who own much of the property in a country.

b Many people who live in squats are too poor to afford accommodation and have taken to squatting as the only possible way of housing themselves.

A CHRISTIAN RESPONSE

Some Christians feel that helping people with housing problems is one way in which they can be real followers of Jesus. They believe that involvement in housing schemes and housing advice centres is one way in which they can help achieve the same kind of equality as the early Christians in Jerusalem were striving for. Others feel that involvement in local politics is the way in which Jesus would want them to respond to the needs of other people. This often involves issues regarding housing.

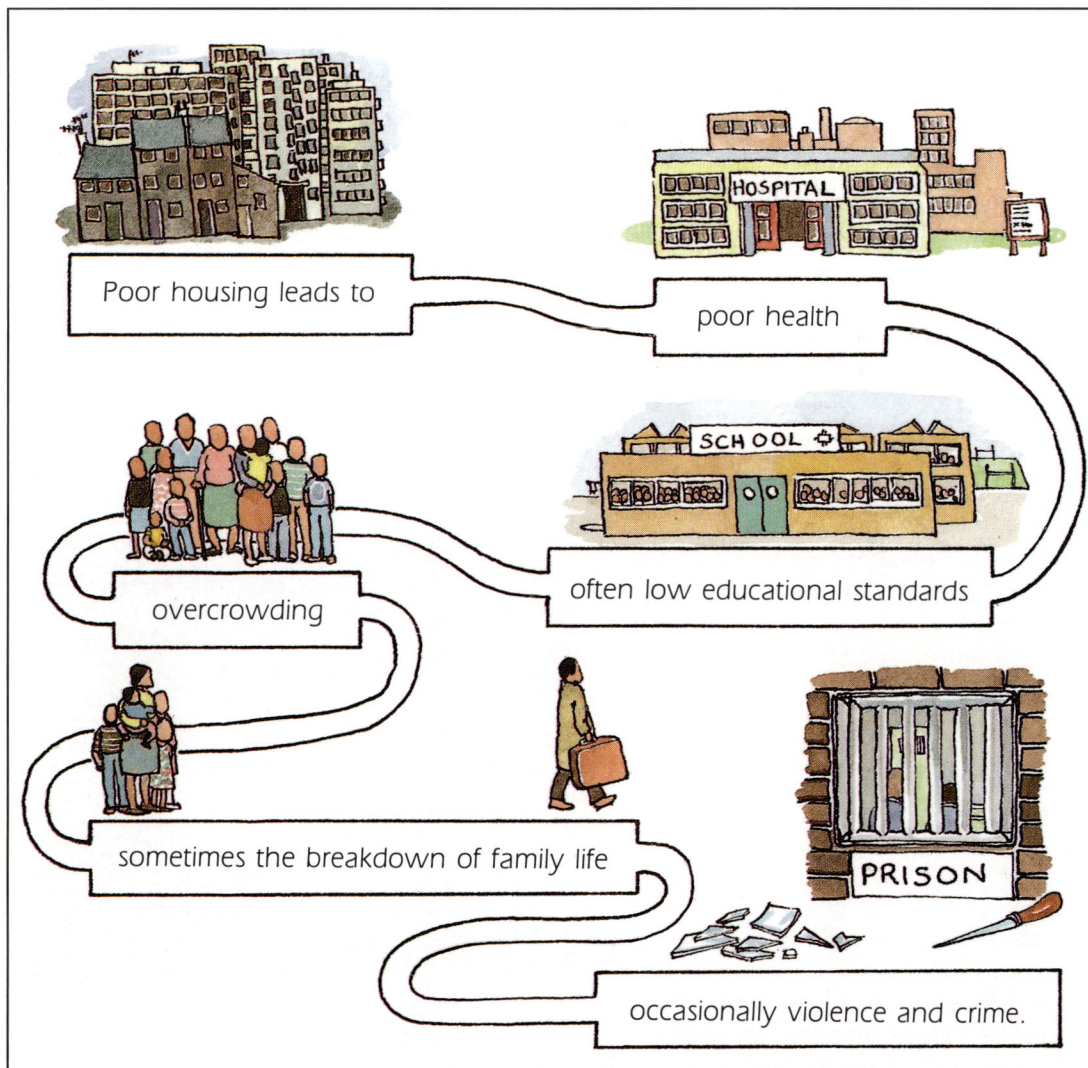

Poor housing leads to

poor health

overcrowding

often low educational standards

sometimes the breakdown of family life

occasionally violence and crime.

1 Quick quiz

a In what ways did the early Christians share their homes? Use Acts 2:43–47 and Acts 4:32–37 to help you.

b Why is a house the most expensive thing most of us will ever buy?

c How much will a building society usually lend?

d What decisions might a couple have to make when they decide to purchase a house?

e What alternatives are there to buying your own home?

f What problems are there in obtaining good rented accommodation?

g Why are there long waiting lists for council property?

h Why might it be difficult for someone living in good rented accommodation to decide to purchase their own property?

i What problems might someone face if their home was demolished to make way for new houses?

j How can housing associations help?

k Which group of Christians is particularly keen on encouraging its members to be involved in housing associations?

l Why might someone need to live in a hostel?

m What reasons might someone have for living in a squat?

n What problems might someone face by living in a squat?

ACTIVITIES

The Conservative government under Mrs Thatcher encouraged people to purchase their own houses. They allowed council tenants the right of purchase too.

Number of dwelling built in the UK, 1967–1987, by type of builder

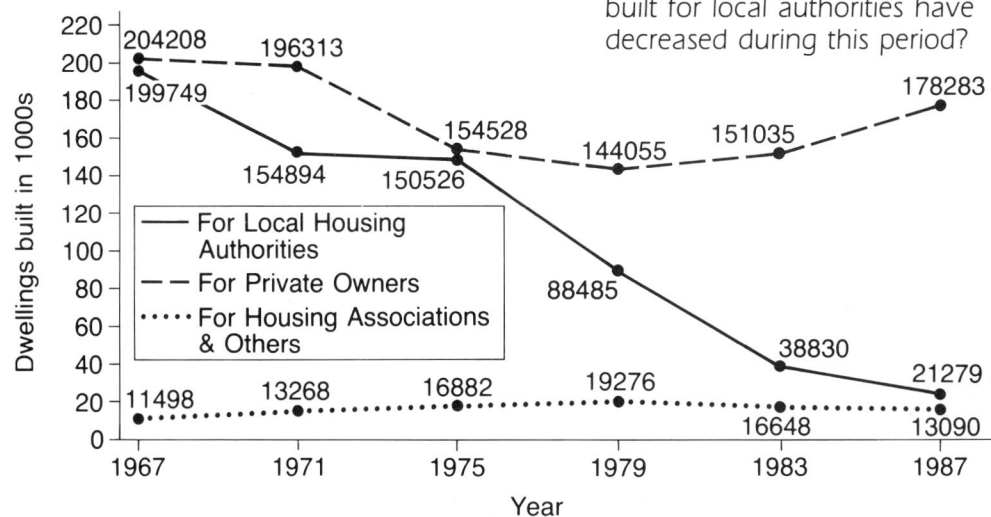

Graph: Dwellings built in 1000s (y-axis) vs Year (x-axis, 1967–1987)

For Local Housing Authorities (solid line): 199749 (1967), 154894 (1971), 150526 (1975), 88485 (1979), 38830 (1983), 21279 (1987)

For Private Owners (dashed line): 204208 (1967), 196313 (1971), 154528 (1975), 144055 (1979), 151035 (1983), 178283 (1987)

For Housing Associations & Others (dotted line): 11498 (1967), 13268 (1971), 16882 (1975), 19276 (1979), 16648 (1983), 13090 (1987)

Source: Annual Abstract of Statistics, 1989

2 Look at the graph on this page.

a Why might the number of houses built for private owners have increased during these years of Conservative government?

b Why might the number of houses built for local authorities have decreased during this period?

HOMES IN THE TIME OF JESUS

Jesus himself spent 30 years of his life in his home in Nazareth. Later, he seems to have lived in Capernaum. We know what the houses were like in Capernaum because remains of them have been found by archaeologists. One of Jesus' best known miracles took place in a house in Capernaum. There was very little rainfall, so the houses there had flat roofs. These were often used for storage, for crafts and household jobs, and for simply relaxing at the end of the day. There was usually a set of steps leading up to the flat roof.

D These houses in Israel are similar to those in in the time of Jesus

3 Read Mark 2:1–12.

a What can you discover about the house in Capernaum by reading this story?

b Do you think the house was one or two storeys? Write down your reason for suggesting this.

Later on, Jesus seems to have spent a lot of time at the home of friends Martha and Mary. They lived at Bethany, just outside Jerusalem. A house has been found there which some people think might have been the one where Martha and Mary lived.

If anyone wanted to make an announcement, they used to shout it from the flat roof of a house. (Joshua 2:6) On the Day of Pentecost (Acts 2), this is probably what Peter was doing when he spoke to the crowd in Jerusalem about Jesus and the Holy Spirit.

Read the story in Acts 2 for yourself.

4 Isaiah 58:7.

'Share your food with the hungry and open your homes to the homeless poor.' In the Bible a home was something to be shared. How might people now share their homes with others?

5 What is really essential?
Make a list of all the things you think are essential in a home.

Clean water.
A room of my own.
Good C.D. Player.
Television.
Telephone.
Washing Machine.

6 Now look at picture E of the shanty home in Jakarta, Indonesia.

E

a Make a list of all the things which are missing from that home.

b Can it still be called a home? Write down some reasons for your answer.

7 a What do you think it might be like to live in those surroundings?

b What would you miss most from your present way of life?

Christian organizations, including Tear Fund and Traidcraft, are active in helping people who live in places like this shanty town. They run self-help schemes to encourage people to use their talents by producing craft goods which can be sold in richer countries. They organize community projects which improve the conditions in which people live.

8 Make a list of the ways in which you think the people of a shanty town might be helped, by:
(i) charities
(ii) governments
(iii) ordinary people.

FIRST SIGHT OF A SHANTY TOWN

I will never forget the first time I saw the shanty town. It was a hot summer, and the hotels were filled with wealthy tourists. There was such a contrast between rich and poor. The rich in their cars rode by and took photographs of the poverty to show the folks back home. I was numbed by it. I found it impossible to take any pictures. It was too horrifying. Although it was hot, the narrow spaces between the houses, (I can't call them streets) were awash with water from washing which was drying on the cardboard and corrugated iron walls of the shelters people had erected for themselves. Bare bottomed babies played in the mud, while other children came up to the cars and passers-by to beg. Inevitably there was no sanitation. There seemed to be so little hope for these people, unless the rest of us were prepared to care in a deeper more passionate way.

G. Weightman.

UNDERCOVER MISSION

After World War 2, a remarkable young priest, called Father Borelli, went to share the lives of some street children in Naples. When they had accepted him, and trusted him as one of themselves, he showed them a house where they could be safe, well-fed and learn to be children again. Christian churches are now very actively involved in providing homes and a purpose in life for such children, particularly in South America.

One hundred million people in the world are homeless.

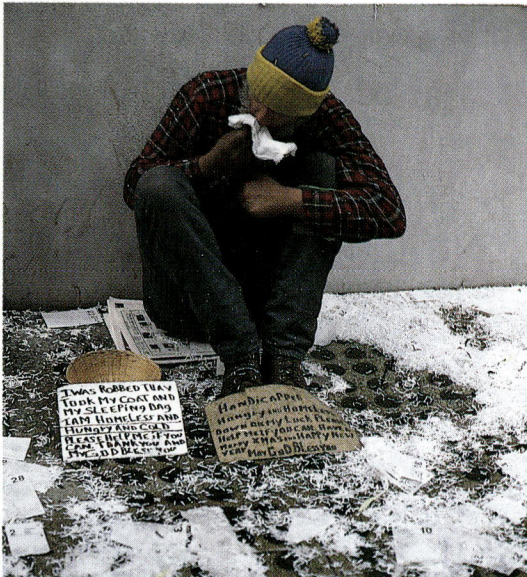

A They sleep on the streets . . .

THIRD WORLD

In the 'Third World', or 'developing world', there are at least 30 million children living on the streets, scraping an existence.

Some homes in these countries are not much better than living on the streets. In the many shanty towns, there is no piped water, no sanitation and no community service like rubbish collection. Few people have any possibility of education, and there are no welfare services. These self-built towns are erected on illegally used land, often owned by someone who has never seen it.

OWNERSHIP OF LAND

In the Third World urban land is often owned by the railway, the army, and in

B . . . on benches . . .

some places, by the Churches who went there as missionaries in the 19th century. Rural land is usually owned by wealthy land owners. Ninety per cent of the world's land is in fact owned by just 3 per cent of the population.

FORCED TO TAKE OVER LAND

Landless and homeless people in the Third World are often forced into squatting. Whereas this usually means taking over a disused building in the richer northern countries, in southern countries it means taking over land and occupying it. Some governments, particularly in South America, are beginning to accept these organized take-overs of land. For example, in Bogota, Colombia, about 60 per cent of the residential land is occupied illegally. The problems of homelessness there are so severe that the legal formalities are being ignored.

In Lima, Peru, there are organized land invasions. Hundreds of homeless families are organized into moving overnight on to a piece of land.

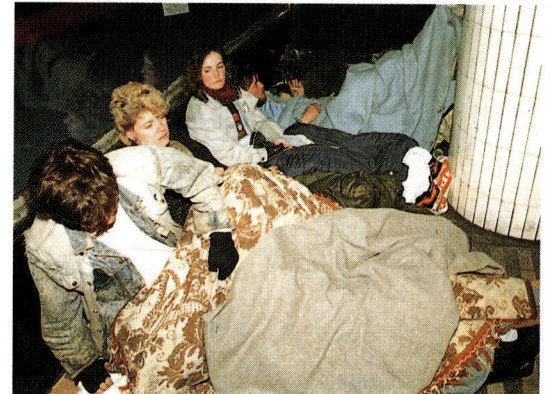

C . . . and in doorways

JESUS

Christians have always had a great deal of sympathy with the homeless. On the night before Jesus was born, Mary and Joseph were looking desperately around Bethlehem to find somewhere for Mary to give birth to Jesus. He began life in a borrowed cradle. Finally he was buried in a borrowed tomb. Throughout his ministry Jesus had no home to call his own. He and his disciples left everything to tell people about the Kingdom of God.

D Hostels for the homeless may be run by Christian organizations

KINGDOM OF GOD

The Kingdom of God, Jesus said, welcomed the poor and the homeless. He wanted everyone to see the needs of these people and to share with them. Every time someone helps someone in need, they should regard it as actually helping Jesus himself (Matthew 25:31–46).

CHRISTIANS MUST HELP

Christians, therefore, ought always to be at the forefront in helping the homeless. This means in every situation. It is often easier to give money to help homeless people in South America or India than to do something about homeless people in Britain. The early Christians tried to distribute things equally, so that everyone's needs were met. This, ideally, is what Christians try to do when a church begins to function as a real family.

In Brazil a bishop was having a new cathedral built. He saw the needs of the people around him, and stopped the work in the cathedral. He transferred the money and the workers to the job of building houses, saying, 'My people need homes first'. This is the same attitude which prompted a church in Kent to send people to Africa to help build houses for a poor Christian community.

The Salvation Army has always been at the forefront of helping homeless people and still provides hostel accommodation for the homeless.

Within the Vatican in Rome there is now a hostel for homeless people. It was begun because Mother Teresa suggested it to the Pope. Intended for the poorest of the poor, it houses 74 homeless people who simply ask for entry at the door of the Vatican.

In the 19th century, Dr Barnado, Lord Shaftesbury and others tried to provide homes and education for homeless children on the streets of London. In various forms their work is continued today.

HOMELESS PEOPLE IN ALL COUNTRIES

The problem of homelessness is severe even in the affluent northern nations. There are thousands of people, many of them teenagers, sleeping rough on the streets of Europe and America. Jesus' challenge to Christians remains the same: if you don't do something for one of these least important people, then you aren't serving me (Matthew 25:44).

ACTIVITIES

Quick quiz

a How many people in the world are thought to be homeless?

b Make a list of the kinds of places where homeless people sleep.

c How many children are there living on the streets?

d Make a list of reasons for so many children being homeless.

e Who owns most of the land in the towns in the Third World?

f Who owns most of the land in the country in the Third World?

g What does occupying a squat usually involve in the poorer southern nations?

h How is it organized in Peru?

i Why do you think that the authorities turn a blind eye to the squatters in Bogota?

j Write down some reaons for Christians being particularly interested in the problems of homelessness.

k Who is welcomed in the Kingdom of God?

l Why should Christians try to help people in need?

m What similarities are there between the Early Church trying to share things equally and the Brazilian bishop who stopped the building of a cathedral?

n What arrangements are there to help homeless people in the Vatican?

o Does it surprise you that there is a problem of homelessness in Europe and the USA? Write down some reasons for your answer.

FURTHER ACTIVITIES

E 'Smokey Mountain' in the Philippines: this rubbish dump is where hundreds of children live and work

1 Brainstorm

a In groups, write down all the reasons you can think of for homeless, unemployed people choosing to live near a rubbish dump.

b Now make a list of the reasons why you think wealthy people living nearby might want to stop them.

c Use your lists to write two newspaper reports. One should be from the point of view of someone who wants the world to know about the difficulties faced by the people living on the rubbish dump. The other one should be from the point of view of outraged wealthy people who want the people who live on the dump moved on.

2 Discuss

Why do you think there are so many shanty towns in the Third World?

Remember
Homelessness is not always the fault of the people who are homeless. Without a job, it is increasingly difficult to get any kind of a home.

3 Something to think about

Why do you think some people
a have to sleep rough?
b choose to sleep rough?

4 Find out

About homelessness in your area.
yes . . . there will be people who are homeless in *your* area, however affluent it might seem.

a You could ask someone from the local branch of Shelter to come and talk to your class. If you decide to do this, you could use a word processor to write a letter inviting them. Make sure you offer them a choice of times to come. It might be possible for them to speak in assembly about homelessness. Make sure that he

ON YOUR NIGHT OUT...

...THINK OF OTHERS ON THEIRS

CRISIS

Working for Homeless People

Please send your donation to: CRISIS · 212 Whitechapel Road London E1 1BJ · Telephone 01 377 0489

F Crisis is another organization that helps homeless people

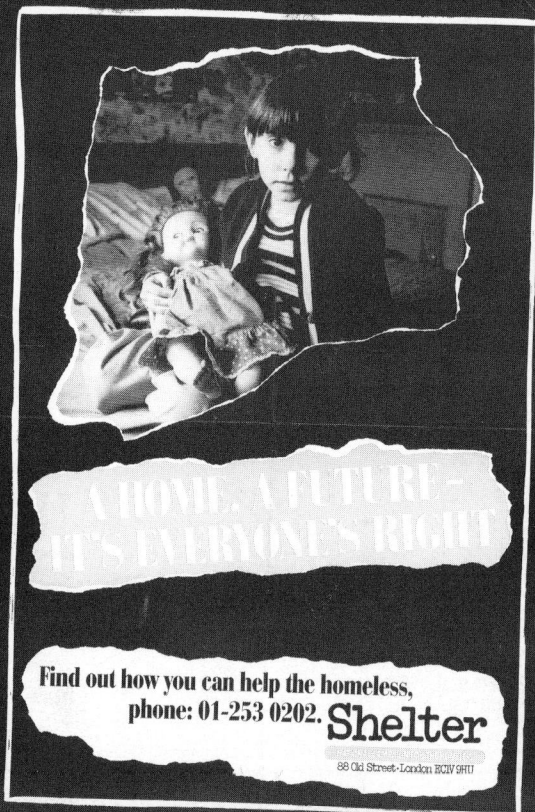

Here is what happened in one school when they decided to help homeless people.

School: Maidstone Girls Grammar School (MGGS), Kent

Subject: Community studies

Leader: Miss Pat McCabe, Deputy Head.

Her background: Anglican Christian who had spent two Christmasses helping the homeless at London's Crisis at Christmas.

Idea: To start a soup run to feed the homeless in the town.

Funding: Initially money offered by Round Table.

Organization: Girls prepare food in the lunch hour three days a week. Other food is donated by shops in the town who sell take-away sandwiches etc. It is distributed to men (very few homeless women) at 7.30 p.m. Only sixth form girls may be involved. They are always closely supervised by an adult. Some people who prepare food never want to go to meet the men. Others prefer to distribute food.

Developments: Clothes, towels etc. are collected by MGGS and feeder primary schools who are now involved in the project. At Christmas they run a Crisis-type open Christmas for any homeless people in the area. About 60 people attend.

Results: Pat McCabe has now retired from her post as Deputy Head Teacher and devotes herself full-time to helping homeless people in Maidstone. She says that the biggest problem facing the men is finding somewhere to wash and clean themselves. She has therefore started a drop-in centre in the local United Reformed Church to meet this need. She goes to court with the men, visits them in prison and in hospital. She has even arranged for them to be reunited with their long lost families. She begs clothes for them and makes sure they get a balanced diet. She breaks up fights, and acts as a friend, counsellor and peacemaker.

A HOME, A FUTURE – IT'S EVERYONE'S RIGHT

Find out how you can help the homeless, phone: 01-253 0202. **Shelter**

88 Old Street·London EC1V 9HU

G Shelter, the National Campaign for the Homeless, works to solve the problem of homelessness

or she knows the age group of the people in the class or school. Make sure that you have planned well so that you have a range of interesting questions to ask.

b If you have a school newspaper, write a report of the visit. This could interest other people in the problems of homelessness and inspire them to find out how they could help. Use a desk top publishing program, if there is one available, to present your report clearly.

5 Read Matthew 25:21–end.

a Do you think the community project described above is doing what Jesus wanted his followers to do?
Write down some reasons for your answer.

b Imagine that you are making a television appeal for money to help these homeless men. Plan a five-minute broadcast. This could include a video of the men themselves, or perhaps an interview with some of the girls involved, as well as a summary of what the project does.

c Design a leaflet which tells people about the problems of homelessness and how they might be able to help. If you have a suitable computer program this could well be done using desk top publishing. If you also have a scanner or digitizer, use this to add some suitable photographs.

WHO ARE REFUGEES?

UN Definition

A person who 'owing to a well founded fear of being persecuted for reasons of race, religion, nationality, membership of a particular social group or political opinion, is outside the country of his nationality, and is unable, or owing to such fear, is unwilling, to avail himself of the protection of that country'.

Refugees are homeless people who are forced to depend on others for their food and shelter. They may have been forced to leave their own countries because of **persecution**, war or **famine**. They have usually chosen the uncertainty of homelessness instead of the certainty of death, torture or starvation. They have been able to carry little with them. Often they have had to leave behind old or sick relations who were not able to make the journey. They have little hope of ever returning in peace to their homeland. They have had to leave all their possessions to face poverty and loss of independence and self respect and to be dependent on others for the most basic necessities of life.

HISTORY

Throughout history there have been refugees. Jacob and his sons went to Egypt in search of food when there was a famine in Canaan. They stayed there, and their descendants eventually became slaves. They were led back to Canaan hundreds of years later by Moses (The book of Exodus).

JESUS

Jesus was still a baby when his parents were warned that King Herod was likely to kill him if they remained in Bethlehem. They too became refugees in Egypt until it was safe to return to their own country.

RELIGIOUS PERSECUTION

Religious persecution has often made people leave their own lands and become refugees elsewhere. The Jews have a long history of moving on when they have been persecuted. This is one reason why they are now scattered in every country of the world.

After the **Reformation**, Christians exiled from their own countries became refugees in other lands. Sometimes they were able to contribute a great deal to the life of the country. Here is Voltaire's description of French Protestant refugees in the late 18th century.

'In the course of three years, nearly 50,000 families left France . . . they brought with them their arts, their manufactures, their wealth . . . art that was henceforth lost to France.'

REFUGEES IN THE WORLD TODAY

In the world today there are six main areas from which refugees come. These are:
Central and South America
Middle East
parts of Africa
Afghanistan
South East Asia
Eastern Europe

When conditions in a country become intolerable, people are often seized by fear and try to leave that country in great numbers.

There were many refugees in Europe after World War 2. They were housed in refugee camps near the borders with the Eastern European countries. Many people who lived in Eastern Europe tried to move to the West to escape the **communist regime** there. From 1961 to 1989 there was a wall across Berlin which was thoroughly guarded to prevent people escaping to the West.

A 'Flight into Egypt' by Fra Angelico

B An Afghan refugee camp

By 1989, the people of East Germany were demanding to be allowed to move to the West and so the wall was eventually removed. Many people moved to the West, where there are still serious problems in trying to cope with so many extra people.

C Breaking through the Berlin Wall

In 1959 'World Refugee Year' highlighted the problems of the 1.2 million refugees in the world. By 1990 there were at least 15 million refugees.

VIETNAMESE BOAT PEOPLE

The Vietnamese people have suffered greatly in the years since World War 2. Many of them have risked their lives to leave the communist areas of North Vietnam. They have crossed the sea in frail boats in attempts to reach Hong Kong. Huge refugee camps have been set up in Hong Kong, and many countries have accepted certain numbers of boat people. However, places cannot be found for all of these people, so many of them are being sent back to North Vietnam.

D Fleeing from Vietnam

Many Vietnamese have been accepted by the United States of America. The Tandy Corporation at Fort Worth, Texas is proud to have employed large numbers of Vietnamese there. They claim they employ 14 different nationalities and help all of them settle down to become Americans.

PAKISTAN

Pakistan has the largest number of refugees in the world. Often the refugee population exceeds that of the local population. There are at least 3 million refugees there.

AFRICA

Half the world's refugees are in Africa. The reasons behind this are continued violence, civil war, the failure of food supplies and the political situation.

TOWARDS A CHRISTIAN VIEWPOINT

'I was a stranger, and you took me in', said Jesus. Christians are bound to ask themselves what Jesus would have wanted them to do about the problem of refugees. They may say, 'I am just one person, I can do nothing', but they can change public opinion. They can write to their MP, or write letters to the press. They can also learn as much as they can about the problems of being a refugee, and they can support the charities which try to help refugees throughout the world.

NOTES/DATABASE

Look up the following words in the glossary. Then use the definitions to make suitable entries for your notebook or database.

Refugee	Reformation
Persecution	Communist regime
Famine	

ACTIVITIES

1 **Quick quiz**

  a Why have refugees often been forced to leave their own countries?

  b Why do refugees usually have very few possessions?

  c Why have they had to leave some of their relations behind?

  d What was the reason for Jacob becoming a refugee in Egypt?

  e Why did Jesus' parents flee to Egypt?

  f How has religious persecution contributed to Jews being scattered all over the world?

  g Which religious refugees was Voltaire describing?

  h How did Voltaire think that they could contribute to the life of a nation?

  i Do you think Voltaire's opinion is still true?

  j Make a list of the main areas of the world where refugees come from.

  k Why have there been so many refugees from Eastern Europe?

  l How many refugees were there in the world by 1990?

  m What problems do Vietnamese trying to escape face?

  n Which country has the greatest number of refugees?

  o What reasons are there for there being three million refugees in Africa?

  p Why should Christians begin to tackle the problem of refugees?

FURTHER ACTIVITIES

DIET NOT ENOUGH TO KEEP CHILD ALIVE, SAYS DOCTOR

UN is blamed for death of refugees

By FIONA BARTON

UP TO 100,000 refugees have died because of the diet provided by an international relief agency, a doctor claimed yesterday.

The United Nations High Commission for Refugees failed to heed repeated warnings from food experts, according to Dr John Seaman of the Save The Children Fund.

At Hartisheik refugee camp in Ethiopia, where a quarter of the children are severely malnourished, the daily handout is 400 grammes of wheat flour.

Supplies of vegetable oil, soya milk, fruit and vegetables, which are supposed to supplement this meagre ration, have not arrived at the camp for months.

Dr Seaman said: 'It is virtually impossible to live

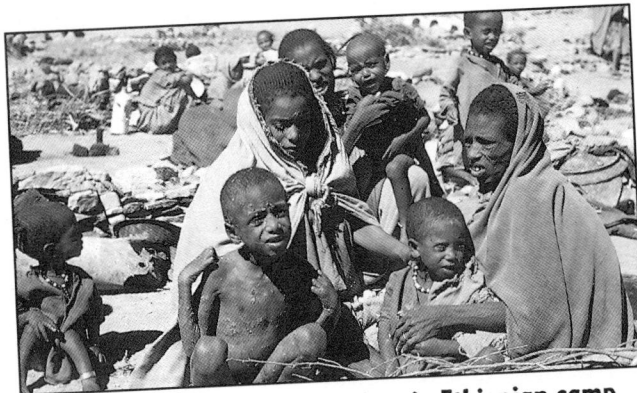

VICTIMS: Mothers and children in Ethiopian camp

on wheat flour in the long run. It isn't a complete diet.

'Even if there is enough of it, it is extremely difficult for a small child to eat enough to keep its body weight up.

'This diet is deficient in a range of nutrients, principally Vitamin C. The result is that they get scurvy and this weakens their resistance to other diseases.

'It is a very defensible estimate that there have been in the order of 100,000 avoidable deaths in refugee camps in East Africa in the last five years alone.'

Scurvy

More than 60,000 refugees at the Hartisheik camp, a

sea of tents housing 230,000 mainly middle-class Somalis who fled across the border to escape civil war, developed scurvy last year. The once proud, healthy men and women who walked for days to find sanctuary have grown thinner, ill and cowed.

The camp, which has become the fourth largest city in Ethiopia, has no electricity or sanitation. It is 35 miles from the nearest water supply and 600 miles from the capital Addis Ababa.

A camera crew for London Weekend Television's Eyewitness programme visited Hartisheik and a documentary about the camp is to be shown at lunchtime today.

A spokesman for the UN Commission, which funnels donations from world governments and has a total budget of $500 million, admitted: 'There are always improvements which could and should be made. But it requires more money.'

Dr Seaman added: 'I have a strong suspicion we could run a quite healthy refugee camp for the same budget.'

THE UNHCR

The United Nations High Commission for Refugees (UNHCR) was set up in 1951 to tackle the problem of stateless and homeless people living in the refugee camps which were mainly on the borders of Eastern Europe. Many of the people had been in the camps since the end of World War 2.

By 1990 there were 15 million refugees in the world. The money to support UNHCR work comes from the richer nations. They also want a say in how the money is spent. However, in 1990 the budget for UNHCR was *cut* by 120 million dollars from 468 million to 348 million dollars.

UNHCR does not help victims of famine or natural disasters. That is the job of other UN agencies. Its task is to aid refugees.

Comment

The television programme *Eyewitness* had also discovered that reports sent from Addis Ababa did not say that food supplies had failed to reach the camp. The reports also failed to mention that many people in the camp were ill.

1 Use the facts in this unit to compile your own in-depth report on refugees.

You could choose to do this as a television report, by making a video, in which case you will need to provide a complete script for your programme. You could take sections from other videos to provide local pictures and edit these together with sections in which members of your class have been either presenters or experts. You will need to make a detailed storyboard. Look carefully at the example of how to produce a storyboard on this page.

You might prefer to produce a booklet explaining about problems faced by refugees. Use a desk top publishing program to prepare this if you have access to a suitable computer.

E Ethiopian refugees

Christians have responded to the needs of refugees with offers of help. Sometimes this has been through sending money. Food aid has also helped, and a number of Christian organizations have set up refugee camps. These try to cater for the physical and spiritual needs of the people. Often Christian organizations set up self-help schemes within the refugee camps as well as funding resettlement schemes. Among the organizations are Christian Aid and CAFOD.

AN EXAMPLE OF A STORYBOARD

	15 sec. LONG SHOT.	Today there are over 15 million refugees.
	10 sec. MEDIUM SHOT.	Over there on the barren desert are the tents in which some of them live.
	12 sec. CLOSE SHOT	Water has to be brought in by lorry from a pipe 35 miles away and is carefully rationed.
	15 sec. CLOSE SHOT.	Wheat flour is the only diet available here. It is hard to keep up body weight by eating wheat flour alone.

2 How would you feel?

Imagine you are about to become a refugee. You have to leave your home in a hurry and can only take a small rucksack of belongings. You may be in danger as you cross the border from your own country. You face uncertainty, and the possibility of never returning to your own country again.

Write a story explaining your escape and your hopes for the future.

Here are some addresses for you to find out more information.

British Refugee Council
Bondway House
3–9 Broadway
London SW8 1SJ

Christian Aid
PO Box No. 100
London SE1 7RT

UNHCR Branch Office
36 Westminster Palace Gardens
Artillery Row
London SW1 1RR

UN Declaration on Human Rights

'The child shall be protected from practices which may foster racial, religious and any other form of discrimination.'

JESUS

Jesus accepted everyone. He showed by his actions that he believed that everyone needed and deserved love. Unlike many of his fellow Jews, his love did not stop at his own country people. He was prepared to show love to men and women of other nationalities. He healed the servant of a Roman Centurion, and the daughter of a Syro-Phoenician woman. He was prepared to spend time chatting to a Samaritan woman who was treated as an **outcast** even by her own villagers. A Samaritan was the hero of one of his stories and shown to be the only character who understood the real meaning of love. (Luke 10:29–37, The Good Samaritan)

Jesus was prepared to love those people who were treated as social outcasts too. He not only ate with tax collectors but even made one of them, Matthew, a disciple. They were hated because they were regarded as traitors

A The many races of the world

. . . they collected taxes on behalf of the Roman government.

MULTI-RACIAL SOCIETY

Jesus was brought up in a **multi-racial** society. The country of Judea was under Roman rule. Among the Jewish population lived many ethnic minorities, including a large number of Greeks. Jesus was no stranger to people of a different colour either. Many Jews were 'berbers', resembling the people of Ethiopia, while others were much lighter in colour. The man who carried Jesus' cross may well have been black. His name was Simon and he came from Cyrene, in Africa.

EQUALS

Jesus treated everyone as equals. He was not interested in a person's racial origins. The Kingdom of God, he said, was for everyone. The qualifications for entrance were nothing to do with **race**. What was needed was for people to do what God wanted. In his last instructions to the disciples (Matthew 28) Jesus told them to baptize people *everywhere*.

THE EARLY CHURCH

There seems to have been little or no colour **prejudice** in Rome. People belonged to different races, and were accepted as equals. In Rome what mattered was citizenship of the Empire. What mattered to Christians was that their citizenship was in heaven. When Paul says everyone is equal, he doesn't even mention colour. 'In Christ there is neither Jew nor Gentile, man nor woman, slave nor free, but everyone is united in Christ.' (Galatians 3:28)

B A breakthrough against prejudice?

DIFFERENT RACES IN BRITAIN

There have been people with different coloured skins in the UK from the time of the Romans, and since the 16th century there have been communities of people with different racial backgrounds. By the 18th century there were 10,000 people from different countries and this figure had doubled by 1920. **Immigrants** with all colours of skin have arrived to settle in the UK. There have been white immigrants, Chinese, Asian, West Indian and African immigrants – people from all over the world and of almost every racial origin. They have often been welcomed as people with skills which are needed.

PREJUDICE

Prejudice, however, can show in two directions. Sometimes it can be on the part of the host nation, when people feel threatened by strangers whose ways they do not understand. It can also come from those immigrants who keep themselves to themselves and preserve their own culture and traditions without regard for the traditions of the host country.

FAITH IN THE CITY

The Church of England prepared a report in 1985 about inner city areas. Here is what it said about attitudes towards ethnic minorities:

'What has concerned us is . . . that far from recognizing that black people are allocated the worst accommodation, many white tenants perceive them as ''jumping the queue'' and receiving favourable treatment. It is crucial that these feelings are understood, for they are closely linked to the racial harassment which has become a disturbing and increasing phenomenon of many urban areas'.

The report *Faith in the city* showed the reality. Christians need to get closer to the truth, this time expressed by the Roman Catholic Church:

'The Church rejects, as foreign to the mind of Christ, any **discrimination** against men or harassment of them because of their race, colour, condition of life or religion.' (*Vatican II*)

When Christians can live by this, then they will be closer to doing what God wants in the world which they believe he created.

NOTES/DATABASE

Look up the following words in the glossary. Then use the definitions to make suitable entries for your notebook or database.

Discrimination	Race
Outcast	Immigrants
Multi-racial	Prejudice

ACTIVITIES

Quick quiz

a Make a list of some of the ways in which Jesus showed that he was prepared to show love to people of every nationality.

b How did Jesus show that he cared about social outcasts?

c In which ways was the society Jesus lived in a 'multi-racial' society?

d What are the qualifications for being part of the Kingdom of God?

e How do we know that there was little racial prejudice in the Roman Empire?

f When did black people first arrive in Britain?

g Where have immigrants to Britain come from?

h Why are members of the host nation sometimes prejudiced against immigrants?

i In which ways might immigrants show prejudice?

j What does the Church of England report *Faith in the City* tell us about the attitude of some white people?

k What is the ideal attitude expressed by the Roman Catholic extract from *Vatican II*?

C Olympic athletes are of all races

2 Read all about it!

a As a group, try to collect as many of this week's newspapers as possible. Cut out and collect all the reports of prejudice, or which are prejudiced themselves, which you can find. Classify them under the headings shown in the chart.

b In the chart, think of a short heading for each story which helps you to classify it.

Decide which parts of each report are primary sources (words of an eye witness) and which are secondary sources (comment from someone else). This could help you to make your own comment on the articles you collect.

c At the end of the week, use the source material you have collected to write an essay called 'Prejudice this week'.

Social prejudice	Racial prejudice	Religious prejudice

FURTHER ACTIVITIES

1 Understand each other

a Are there any races except your own in your school?

b Make a list of other ethnic groups represented at your school.

c Arrange to interview, preferably on audio tape, people from different ethnic groups. These could be combined to make a radio-style chat show. If you have a multi-cultural centre near your school, arrange a visit. They might be interested to include a copy of your radio show among their resources.

2 Your computer could be useful in producing a multi-cultural magazine in which people from different ethnic or religious groups provide articles. These could help you all to understand one another better.

3 Look up the following Bible verses:

Matthew 23:8–11
Galatians 3:20–28
Acts 10:34f
Matthew 5:9
Romans 12:10–21

Now discuss in a group how these verses can help people work out a Christian attitude towards living in harmony with each other.

SOUTH AFRICA

Anti-apartheid organizations are seizing the education initiative.

Mary Castle reports from London

In the week of Nelson Mandela's release, anti-apartheid organizations are pressing ahead with demands to reform black education.

The recently-unbanned National Education Co-ordinating Committee has asked the Government to allow black children to fill 300,000 vacancies in white schools.

The threat of school closures caused by the declining white birth-rate has already forced the hand of parents and students in Cape Town where 30 schools have voted to admit black pupils.

And in Johannesburg, the All Schools for All People Campaign wants the Government to admit its education policy has failed and to open schools in white urban areas to black children. Johannesburg's white population is declining at a rate of about 1,600 a year and 206 schools have closed.

Mr Ihron Rensburg, general secretary of the NECC and executive member of the United Democratic Front, is at the forefront of the struggle for better education. He has been tortured, detained for almost three years and gone on hunger strike in pursuit of his demands.

If the Government agrees to his organization's request it will bring some relief to black children currently sharing books and desks between five in classes of 80 to 90.

In the secondary sector, the average teacher-pupil ratio is 1:52; for their white peers it is 1:15.

But reconstruction in post-apartheid South Africa will be costly. Many black South Africans receive no education at all and 60 per cent are illiterate. To date South Africa spends five times more on a white child's education than on a black child's.

The NECC estimates that the cost of bringing "Third World" schools and technical colleges up to First World standards will be about 21 billion rands (£3.5 bn).

The money would pay to bring electricity to the 80 per cent of black schools without it, cover maintenance and running costs, reduce class sizes, meet the teacher training bill, and create space for the annual influx of 220,000 black children.

Much of the student unrest in recent years has focused on a curriculum that prepares black children for a life of manual or semi-skilled work.

Forty times more white students than black pass maths in their final school year.

Forty per cent of white teachers have a degree and teaching certificate compared with only 4 per cent of black staff.

APARTHEID

South Africa has had a long history of 'apartheid'. This means the separation of races, imposed by the whites. Schools have been separate, as well as areas in which people live, and even places of entertainment. This is slowly changing.

4 Read the report of black children being admitted to some white schools.

a Do you think this will help the next generation of South Africans to be less prejudiced?

b What kinds of thing do you think people need to learn about in schools to help them avoid being racially or religiously prejudiced?

D Schools can help to fight prejudice

PEOPLE WHO HAVE FOUGHT FOR EQUALITY

Nelson Mandela

He is a black South African leader who spent 28 years in prison. He was imprisoned for his opposition to apartheid. He was released in 1990 and continues to work for black rights in his country.

Mahatma Gandhi

He fought for civil rights for people in Africa before returning to India to continue the fight. He said his religion included the best from Hinduism, Islam and Christianity although he always remained a devout Hindu.

Mother Teresa

Until her retirement in 1990, Mother Teresa fought against poverty and disease wherever she met them. She helped people irrespective of race or religion, and devoted her life to helping the 'poorest of the poor'. Her work continues through the religious orders which she founded.

Trevor Huddleston

He spent some years fighting against the 'pass laws' in South Africa which meant that black and Coloured people had to take a special identification pass with them wherever they went and could be asked to present it at any time. They were not allowed in the same places as white people. He wrote a book called *Naught for your comfort* which told the world of the plight of black and Coloured people in South Africa. He continued the fight against racism as a bishop in London's East End.

5 a In groups, find out more about these people and how they have contributed to encouraging people to live in harmony.

b Choose one of these people and prepare a talk about them. If you are able to do so, use an overhead projector in the presentation of your talk. Prepare some interesting overhead projector transparencies to help you to illustrate your talk. Make your words and drawings bold and easy to understand, and remember, humour always helps to keep people interested.

Deuteronomy 19:19–21

'You shall treat him as he intended to treat his fellow . . . an eye for an eye and a tooth for a tooth.'

Matthew 5:38–40

Jesus said, 'You have learned that they were told an eye for an eye and a tooth for a tooth. Do not set yourself against the man who wrongs you. If someone slaps you on the right cheek, turn and offer him your left.'

Gandhi

'An eye for an eye, and we shall soon be blind.'

PACIFISM

Amongst the Christians who believe that all war and violence is wrong are many **Quakers**. Like other believers in non-violence, they consider that violence solves nothing. War and violence are essentially evil in themselves. Therefore it follows that using evil to prevent evil is wrong. It can only lead to short-term solutions.

Pacifism and **non-violence** are sometimes a most difficult path to follow. There are many situations in which it seems natural to react with violence. Pacifists believe that there is a better way. They point to the fact that there have been countless wars and still peace seems unobtainable. Pacifism, they say, has yet to be put to the test.

NON-VIOLENCE

Many Christians have been inspired to learn about the methods of non-violent protest from Mahatma Gandhi, an Indian Hindu leader. He lived in India in the early part of the 20th century. He believed that non-violent solutions were the only ones which would be effective. These included the use of peaceful protest, and sometimes even refusing to eat until a problem was solved.

MARTIN LUTHER KING

An admirer of Gandhi's methods was Dr Martin Luther King, an American Civil Rights leader and Baptist minister. Like Gandhi, he believed that in situations where people were powerless, the only method of achieving their demands was through non-violent protest.

BUS BOYCOTT

Martin Luther King used this method very effectively when he organized a bus **boycott**. The buses in Montgomery, Alabama, USA were **segregated**. This meant that certain seats were reserved for white people only. In December 1955, Mrs Rosa Parkes, who was black, sat down in one of the white seats. She was asked to move by a white passenger. She refused and was arrested. Dr King and other black Church ministers organized a boycott of the buses. This meant that for 18 months in Montgomery, no black person went by bus. Immense hardship followed as many people had to get up very early to walk several miles to work. Eventually the bus boycott worked. Buses were no longer segregated. Peaceful protest had won. Other public places were also opened to black people. Soon similar non-violent methods were used by Dr King and his followers to secure changes in the law which gave black Americans the vote.

PEACEFUL PROTESTS AGAINST NUCLEAR WEAPONS

There have been many peaceful protests against the use of nuclear weapons. Amongst these was that made by the Greenham Common women. They camped for years outside the American air bases in the UK, protesting at the siting of American nuclear weapons in this country. Often these non-violent protests ended in violence, which was directed against the protesters. Women

A Protesting peacefully in South Africa

B Women set up a peace camp at Greenham Common to protest about nuclear weapons

who sat down in the path of lorries loaded with missiles were dragged away and sometimes hurt.

TOWARDS A CHRISTIAN ATTITUDE

It is quite difficult to work out a genuinely Christian attitude towards non-violence. Paul commands Christians to be subject to the governing authorities, because they are appointed by God. (Romans 13:1f) However, if the authorities are clearly working against what Christians see as the purposes of God, then this raises the question of whether Christians should stand up for what they believe. Jesus said, 'Do not think that I have come to bring peace on earth: I have not come to bring peace, but a sword.'

It is the task of every individual to work out what they believe to be right. The balance of evidence from the Bible seems to be that it is right to be on the side of truth, even if it means going against the governing authorities. Non-violent protest could be argued as being the most Christian solution in circumstances where people are powerless.

C 'Meet hate with love'

MEET HATE WITH LOVE

One night Martin Luther King came home to discover a bomb had exploded outside his house. Many of his followers wanted to respond violently. This is what he said:
'If you have weapons, take them home. We cannot solve this problem through violence. We must love our white brothers no matter what they do to us. We must make them know that we love them. Jesus still cries out: "Love your enemies." This is what we must live by. We must meet hate with love.'

NOTES/DATABASE

Look up the following words in the glossary. Then use the definitions to make suitable entries for your notebook or database.

Pacifism	Boycott
Non-violence	Segregation
Quakers	

ACTIVITIES

1 **Quick quiz**

a Which group of Christians have many members who believe that all war is wrong?

b Why do Quakers believe that war can only lead to short-term solutions?

c What reasons can you suggest for thinking that pacifism and non-violence are difficult paths to follow?

d Who was Dr Martin Luther King?

e Whose methods were admired by Martin Luther King?

f What were these methods?

g Why was Rosa Parkes arrested?

h What did Dr King and the black community do after her arrest?

i What was the result of the bus boycott in Alabama?

j Why were the Greenham Common women protesting?

k Why do you think that non-violent protesters sometimes get hurt?

l Why do you think it is difficult to work out a genuinely Christian attitude towards non-violence?

m In what circumstances do you think non-violent protest could be effective?

n Why did Martin Luther King say 'Meet hate with love'?

PACIFISM AND NON-VIOLENCE

FURTHER ACTIVITIES

1 How do you respond?

a If someone ducks you at the swimming pool, how do you react?

b If someone ducked a friend who could not swim, how would you react?

c If someone tells lies about you, what do you do?

d If you were being bullied at school, what might you do?

e If someone else was being bullied, what do you think you would do?

f Why do you think you might respond in these ways?

Gandhi said:

'In non-violence the masses have a weapon which enables a child, a woman, or even a decrepit old man, to resist the mightiest government successfully.'

2 a Copy and complete the following chart. Put all the advantages of violence in the first column, and all the advantages of non-violence in the second column.

Advantages of violence	Advantages of non-violence

b Which method do you think is the most effective, and why?

3 Over to you

Are there any circumstances in which you feel that you would be prepared to join in a non-violent protest? Why?

PICTURE THIS!

5 a What have all the pictures got in common?

b Write an appropriate caption for each picture.

D

E

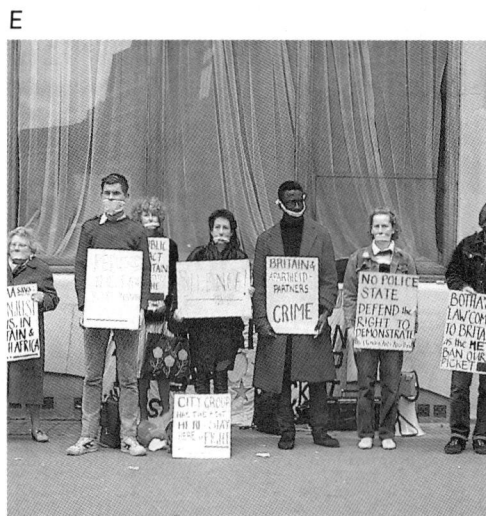

4 Something to think about

Jesus was falsely accused, and he said nothing in his own defence.

c What do you think the people involved hope to achieve in each case?

d In which types of situation do you think non-violent protest would be appropriate?

KEEP FREE TRANSPORT FOR LONDONS' PENSIONERS

F

GREENPEACE IN THE ANTARCTIC

Greenpeace are trying to establish a scientific base on Antarctica. Two successful winters have been spent there by a research team who have been working on seawater analysis and satellite communications. They want Antarctica to become a world wildlife park. They believe very strongly that this is important for world weather patterns, and for preserving the beauty and balance of this wilderness.

The French are building an airstrip in Antarctica, destroying five islands. Greenpeace wished to protest at what they see as a misuse of Antarctica.

The construction of the French airstrip devastated penguin colonies and disturbed offshore life. Greenpeace protested by trying to occupy the airstrip site to stop work until journalists were able to tell the story to the world.

The French construction crews attacked the tent set up by Greenpeace. The construction workers, independently of the French site commander, decided to remove the Greenpeace group by force. They successfully used heavy digging equipment to do this. The press interest in this was intense everywhere in the world. French scientists agreed that the French were breaking the Antarctic treaty by their disregard for the surrroundings and the wildlife. Greenpeace had successfully drawn the attention of the world to the actions of the French.

Greenpeace hope, by being established as an international agency working in Antarctica, to have a voice in Antarctic treaty negotiations.

Some Christians feel that they can express their Christian commitment on important issues by being members of organizations such as Greenpeace. Other Christians are opposed to this.

G Greenpeace protestors in Antarctica

6 a Why were Greenpeace in Antarctica?

b What are the French trying to do there?

c Why are Greenpeace protesting against the French?

d Was their protest non-violent?

e Who started the violence?

f Did Greenpeace achieve their objectives?

g How do Christians feel about organizations such as Greenpeace?

7 Imagine you were one of the journalists accompanying the Greenpeace expedition. Write the story about this event which you would send back to your paper in Europe or America.

8 Now imagine you are one of the French construction workers whose job was delayed by the Greenpeace occupation. Write a report for your bosses in France explaining why you chose to attack the Greenpeace team using heavy digging equipment.

Jesus said 'He sent me to bring good news to the poor, to announce freedom to people in captivity, to restore sight to the blind, to set free people who are oppressed, and to proclaim the coming of the Kingdom of God.' Luke 4:18f

CHRISTIAN ATTITUDES

Some Christians think that Christians should not be involved in politics. They believe that Christianity deals with spiritual and moral values. They are concerned with worshipping God and encouraging people to lead holy lives. Other Christians believe that worship is not complete without being involved in improving the conditions of life for people who are poor and oppressed. This can sometimes involve people in a political struggle.

A Orphans suffered under the Ceausescu regime

SOCIAL ACTION IN HISTORY

There have always been Christians who saw a need to work out their faith in this practical way. It was because of his Christian faith that a bishop called William Wilberforce fought a political struggle in the 19th century to abolish the **slave trade**. In 19th century London, **evangelical** Christians were among the **reformers** who worked to establish homes for the many children who lived on the streets. These included Dr Barnado and Lord Shaftesbury. They believed that Jesus is always on the side of the poor and oppressed, and that it was their duty as Christians to fight to improve conditions for these people.

Father Gustavo Gutierrez, a South American Roman Catholic priest, said 'The poverty of the poor is not a summons to alleviate their plight with acts of generosity, but rather a compelling obligation to fashion an entirely different social order.'

EVIL REGIMES

In some countries of the world today, there is a great division in society between the ruling classes and the poor. Christians have seen that poor people may be exploited and oppressed by governments. Sometimes these governments are led by army officers. Usually the government is kept in place by the power of the army, and many people live in fear.

ROMANIA

The Ceausescu regime in Romania was one of these evil **regimes**. When the government fell in 1989, the rest of the world saw the horror of the conditions in which many people had lived. People all over the world were shocked at the condition of children in orphanages. Sometimes mentally handicapped, they were kept naked and herded into huge

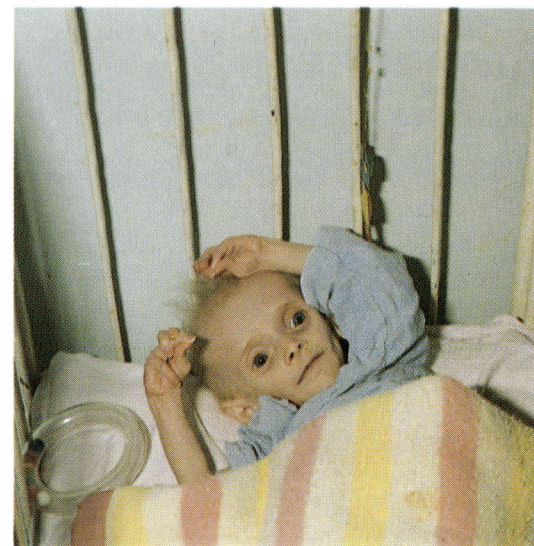

B Why are so many children dying of AIDs in Romania?

cots even when quite old. The regime had said that there was no problem of AIDS in the country as it was a Western disease which was the result of Western social corruption. It had no place within a communist state. No blood was screened for AIDS and so hundreds of children were probably given contaminated blood. The world was driven to compassion by the pictures of hundreds of dying babies suffering in the advanced stages of AIDS.

It is not surprising that some Christians were amongst the first to speak out against this regime, and to be actively involved in its downfall.

SOUTH AMERICA

In South America the Church has been active in drawing the world's attention to injustices caused by some governments. Many Christians, including bishops of the Roman Catholic Church, believe that the gospel demands they stand up and fight against poverty, injustice and the exploitation of the poor.

The lack of basic human rights for ordinary people has caused many to speak fearlessly against repressive governments. Sometimes these Christians

C This homeless child is a victim of a repressive regime in South America

have been involved in fighting against the armed forces. In South America, this movement has become known as **Liberation Theology**. Here is how one South American Roman Catholic priest, Father Camillo Torres, explained why he was prepared to fight.
'I believe that the revolutionary struggle is appropriate for the Christian. Only by changing the conditions of our country can we enable men to practise love for each other.'

NOTES/DATABASE

Look up the following words in the glossary. Then use the definitions to make suitable entries for your notebook or database.

Slave trade   Regime
Evangelical   Liberation Theology
Reformers

ACTIVITIES

1 **Quick quiz**

a How did Jesus describe his work in Luke 4:18f?

b Why do you think that some Christians believe it is wrong for Christians to be involved in politics?

c What reasons might a Christian have for believing it to be right to be involved in a political struggle?

d Why did people like Dr Barnado and Lord Shaftesbury fight to improve conditions in 19th century London?

e What methods have some governments used to exploit poor people?

f How did the rest of the world find out about conditions in Romania?

g In which ways have Christians in South America been active?

h What is this South American movement called?

POLITICS IN THE TIME OF JESUS

Politics were both dangerous and violent in the time of Jesus. The Romans occupied Judea, the country where Jesus lived. Their powerful army was used to maintain law and order. Many Jews resented the presence of the Romans.

There was a revolutionary group called the Zealots who were prepared to fight guerilla warfare to undermine the Roman army. One of Jesus' disciples was a member of this group. The Zealots expected God to send a military leader to drive out the Romans.

Jesus was interested in improving the quality of life and bringing in the Kingdom of God. He was not afraid to challenge the authorities. He showed himself to be on the side of the poor, of outcasts and other disadvantaged members of society. He worked unceasingly to try to make people aware of each others' needs. He expected people to work out their duty to serve God by serving each other and meeting each others' needs.

WANTED
DEAD OR ALIVE
FOR CRIMES AGAINST THE STATE

For telling people their rights, including telling them that they do not need to be in captivity any longer. Unlawfully healing blind people. Giving hope to people who are suffering from oppression.
JESUS OF NAZARETH
IS SPREADING UNREST AND SEDITION

2 **Discuss**

Do you think Jesus would have been prepared actually to fight against an evil government? What other kind of action might he have taken?

FURTHER ACTIVITIES

POLICE FILE

PROFILE OF FATHER CAMILLO TORRES

Name:	Camillo Torres
Date of Birth:	1930
Nationality:	Columbian
Occupation:	Roman Catholic Priest
Marital Status:	Single
Politics:	Founded illegal United Front of Columbian People (not supported by Catholic Church)
Other Information:	Believed that the division of wealth in Columbia was wrong. Therefore became involved in politics to try to create fairer society. Believed that Government would crush any non-violent protest.
Crime:	Starting riots, making peasant population aware of basic human rights. Persuading other priests to join guerilla movement and to fight against the government.

Involved in many fights against the police and government troops. Suspected of having killed many police and soldiers, as well as inciting others to kill. |
| **File Closed:** | 1966 Killed in small skirmish against government troops.

NOTE: Body was buried in a secret grave. Authorities fear he might be regarded as a martyr and saint by ignorant peasants. The authorities suspect that the Nicaraguan revolution in 1979 was inspired by Torres' example. The regime in Nicaragua was overthrown by a movement in which priests and bishops were involved in fighting. |

1 Use the information in the profile of Father Camillo Torres to write an entry for an encyclopedia explaining his importance.

ARCHBISHOP DESMOND TUTU

D Archbishop Desmond Tutu is at the centre of the political struggles in South Africa

Another person who has been inspired by Liberation Theology is Archbishop Desmond Tutu. He has usually used non-violent methods. During a non-violent march in Soweto in 1976, 600 blacks were shot dead by the authorities. He believes that Christianity involves working for justice and equality. This has often brought him into conflict with the authorities. He has been at the forefront of the political struggle to free South Africa from apartheid, and to create a more equal and just society there.

Desmond Tutu regards the Bible as 'the most revolutionary book ever written'. Some people say that the only reason he is still alive is that he is so well known throughout the world.

In 1984 Desmond Tutu was awarded the Nobel Peace Prize. He has constantly spoken out against apartheid, describing it as evil and unchristian. In 1986 he became South Africa's first black archbishop.

'Christian worship can never let us be indifferent to the needs of others, to the cries of the hungry, of the naked and the homeless, of the sick and the prisoner, of the oppressed and the disadvantaged.'
(Sermon 1979, 'Divine Intervention', Desmond Tutu.)

2 Interview

Plan an interview with Desmond Tutu.
What questions would you ask him about his beliefs?
How do you think he would answer your questions?

3 Something to think about

a Is there any situation in your own country which you would like to change?

b Make a list of anything you feel that it is important to change. The photographs on this page may give you some ideas.

F Abuse of the environment

4 Discuss

Imagine that you are a Member of Parliament. You have the possibility of introducing a new law. Design this new law. It should benefit the people who live in your country.

Some groups are involved in political struggles in Britain. They include CND (the Campaign for Nuclear Disarmament); Life, the anti-abortion group; groups opposing the use of animal skins for clothes, or opposing the use of animals for non-medical experiments.

5 Find out about one of the above groups and the way in which it tries to use political methods to change the law.

G Pollution

E Homelessness

The Old Testament tells the story of the people of Israel. Much of that story is concerned with the possession of the land of Israel, often called Canaan at the time. The story dates back to the second millenium BCE.

EARLY SETTLEMENT

A group of tribes known as the Israelites returned to the land of Canaan after a long absence as immigrant workers in Egypt. They wished to settle once again in an area which they believed their ancestors had left some centuries earlier. By that time, other tribes had settled there and built towns, planted crops and established defences.

Much of the early part of the Old Testament is concerned with the struggle to regain a foothold in the land. It is therefore the story of battles between the Israelites and the other tribes. It also explains how Israel saw itself among the nations. It shows how the people of Israel went on believing that their God led them and guided them through every stage of their lives.

The problem for Christians lies in the very warlike nature of some of the stories in the Old Testament. It is important to see these stories as the products of their own time, and to realize that the Israelites believed that God was actually with them, leading them into battle.

Much of the warlike material really deals with the question of obedience. It sometimes seems as though there is a very simple choice facing the people of Israel. If they obey God, and do what he wishes, then everything will go well for them, including battles. If they disobey God's wishes, then everything ends in disaster.

PROBLEMS OF PEACE

The writer of the book of Deuteronomy sees that problems will face the Israelites in times of peace. When they finally live in houses and farm land which they have inherited, then they will forget about God (Deuteronomy 8). Christians believe that the lessons learned by Israel, and written down in the Bible, about war and peace and about obeying God have a relevance for Christians in every generation.

EXILE

Later in the Old Testament the people of Israel, by this time called the Jews, have to face the difficulties of being a conquered nation. Some of the people were taken away to Babylon as hostages. This was a different kind of war, in which the people were dominated by a nation which followed a different religion. As hostages, they learned to cope with the problems of following their religion in a strange land.

ARMIES OF OCCUPATION

Like many other people, the Jews faced many years of being dominated by the Greeks and then by the Romans. There were armies of occupation within Israel, and the people had to keep laws which were made far away, first of all in Greece and then in Rome. Faced with armies which were made up of people whose religion was totally different from their own, the people of Israel were forced once again to look closely at their own belief in God. They went on believing that their God was one who loved and guided his people, whatever difficulties they might be facing.

THE MESSIAH

It is not surprising then that the Jews, who had faced so much defeat in battle, began to look towards an idealistic situation in which a great military leader would save them from the army of occupation. Others took a view which suggested that the Messiah, when he

A 'Monument for a devastated city', Rotterdam

came, would be a man of peace, a teacher of religious truth. The little strip of land we call Israel had been fought over so often that the issues of war and peace had been very thoroughly considered.

CHRISTIAN VIEWS

The Bible is the source of Christian ideas of morality, but there are problems for Christians who want to sort out their personal ideas about war and peace from the Bible.

There certainly are wars in the Bible. The New Testament period was dominated by Roman military rule. Some ideas about being a Christian come from ideas about being a soldier (Ephesians 6:10–19). Jesus himself seemed to be a man of peace, saying nothing in his own defence at his trial. Jesus said that he left a gift of a unique kind of peace with his followers. He also said that he didn't come to bring peace but a sword.

PACIFISM

Some Christians have wished to be pacifists. They have wanted to say that war is always wrong. Amongst these are the Quakers. Some Christians in other denominations also maintain this courageous viewpoint. Other Christians believe that there are circumstances where it is right to fight against evil with whatever means are available, including full-scale war.

WAR CAUSED BY RELIGION

Perhaps the saddest of all wars are those in which people take sides according to the religion which they belong to. Sometimes this has divided families and caused immeasurable suffering and hardship.

THE EFFECTS OF WAR

It is impossible to measure the suffering and sadness caused by war. Often the people who get hurt are not even involved in the fight. Sometimes almost a whole generation of young men is wiped out. In some places of the world there are young people growing up who have never known what it is like to live in a country where there is peace.

In many terms, the costs of war are enormous. The world spends more than £1 million each minute on defence. This seems an especially large amount when you realize it would cost far less to supply everyone in the world with clean water, food, health care and housing.

In times of war, the cost in human terms is unimaginable. Millions of people are injured, tortured or killed. The effects of nuclear and chemical weapons are

borne by the next generation as well. Those who fight in a war, their families and all people living in a war zone suffer both physical and mental damage from war.

ACTIVITIES

1 **Quick quiz**

a What is much of the Old Testament concerned with?

b Why did the Israelites return to settle in the land of Canaan?

c Why did the Israelites need to fight battles?

d What is one of the problems which Christians face when reading stories of battles in the Old Testament?

e What is one of the questions which much of the warlike material actually deals with?

f What problem faces the Israelites in times of peace (according to Deuteronomy)?

g Why were the Jews taken to Babylon as hostages?

h What problems did the Jews face in Babylon?

i What were some of the problems faced by the Jews when they were ruled by the Romans?

j What were some of the views about the Messiah?

k What are some of the things which the New Testament says about war and peace?

l What might a pacifist believe?

AN OLD TESTAMENT BATTLE

The story of David and Goliath is well known. Make sure of the details by reading I Samuel:17.

2 a Write a letter from David applying for the job of fighting the Giant, Goliath of Gath. Use verse 34 to help you write down David's special qualifications for thinking he could tackle Goliath.

b This battle was obviously a great victory from the Israelite point of view, and a great defeat for the Philistines. Write *two* news reports. One of these should be for an Israelite newspaper, and the other for a Philistine newspaper. They should report the event from the two different points of view.

SITUATION VACANT

ONLY THE BRAVEST NEED APPLY.

One day job only . . .

Generous Pension paid to family

**Task:
To kill
GOLIATH OF GATH**

Apply in person to
King Saul

3 This story would also make an excellent cartoon strip. In pairs, work out a series of pictures which would explain the whole story. Make sure you also think of some interesting dialogue to put in the speech bubbles. Use the words in the Bible story to help you to do this.

WAR AND PEACE

FURTHER ACTIVITIES

PUT ON THE WHOLE ARMOUR OF GOD

Look carefully at Ephesians 6:10–19

1 Copy and complete the chart.

  a What does Paul say that Christians are fighting against?

  b Why does he tell Christians to 'put on the whole armour of God'?

  c Why do you think that Paul compares being a Christian with fighting in an army?

  d What circumstances can you think of in which a Christian might be called upon to fight the battle Paul is talking about?

Armour	Meaning
Belt	
Breastplate	
Sandals	
Shield	
Helmet	
Sword	

B A soldier in the war between Iran and Iraq

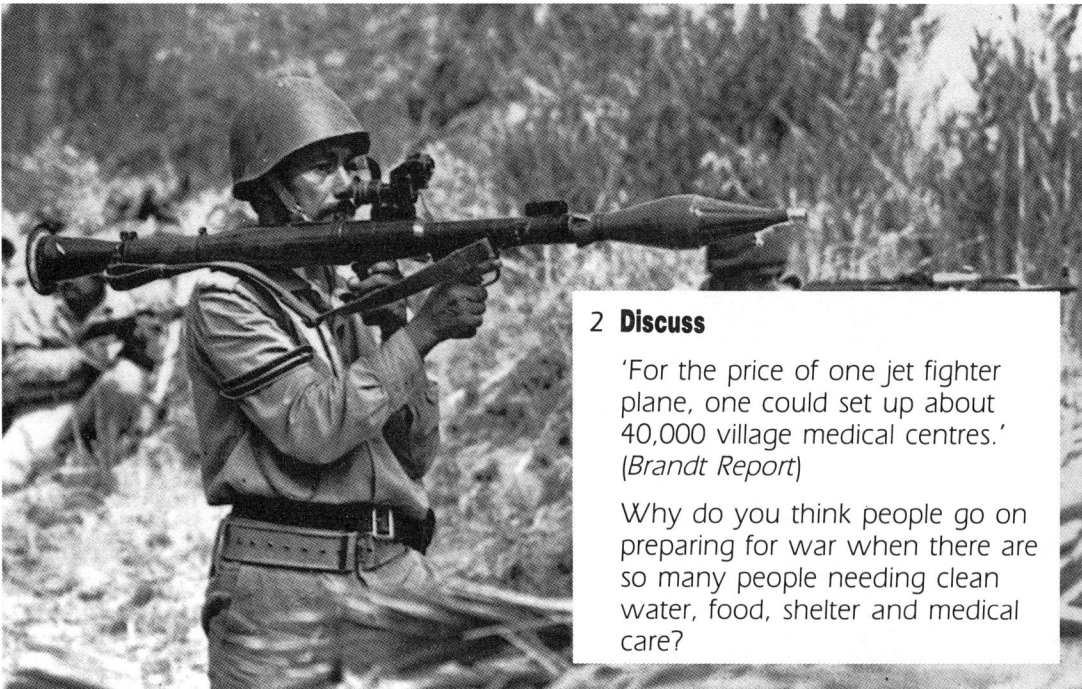

2 Discuss

'For the price of one jet fighter plane, one could set up about 40,000 village medical centres.' (*Brandt Report*)

Why do you think people go on preparing for war when there are so many people needing clean water, food, shelter and medical care?

Methodist Statement on Peace and War.
(Declarations and Statements)

'All Christians agree that war is evil. Some believe that it is, therefore, in every circumstance to be rejected by the followers of Christ. Others believe that there are situations in which waging of war is inevitable as the choice of the lesser of two admitted evils.'

3 What do you think?

CIVIL WAR IN LEBANON

Some of the most difficult of wars to understand are civil wars. There has been civil war in Lebanon since April 1975 when a busload of Palestinians was ambushed by the Marionites, a Christian group in Lebanon. These people were being sent by the busload out of Jordan by King Hussein. Some were sent to Israel and some to the Lebanon. Their presence shifted the balance of power in the Lebanon.

The French, who had previously ruled Lebanon, left a situation in which the majority group held the balance of political power. These were the Marionite Christians. The Palestinians who arrived were Shi'ite Moslems and began to agitate for political power. This (in very over-simplified terms) sparked off the war in Lebanon.

Bombing became a nightly occurrence. Beirut became a city which knew nothing but war. Looting was common as shops and properties were bombed.

The country had previously been rich and prosperous. The biggest casualties in this war have been the ordinary people. The economy of the country is in shreds. There is no industry and little agriculture left. Tourists no longer dare come to Lebanon. Children are growing up who have never known any kind of life but war. They are growing up with hatred of other religious groups, seeing themselves as Marionites (Christians), or Shi'ites (Moslems), or one of the other 15 religious groupings in Lebanon. They have been denied the possibility of a real childhood, and of growing up without knowing terror and hatred.

C Children in Beirut have grown up with war

4 a What was the first event in the Lebanese war?

b Which religious groups were involved in the first skirmishes?

c Write a paragraph about what it might be like to grow up in Beirut during the civil war.

d If you were a Marionite Christian living in Beirut, how would you feel about your Shi'ite neighbours?

e What do you think Jesus' attitude would have been? (Use Luke 10 to help you.)

THANK GOD WHO SAVED US

Veterans of World War 2 meet each year to remember how they were rescued from the beaches at Dunkirk by a flotilla of little ships. In 1990, many of the little ships re-enacted the scene, in a remembrance activity called 'Operation Dynamo'. The central part of the annual act of remembrance is the two services, one at Dunkirk, one at De Panne.

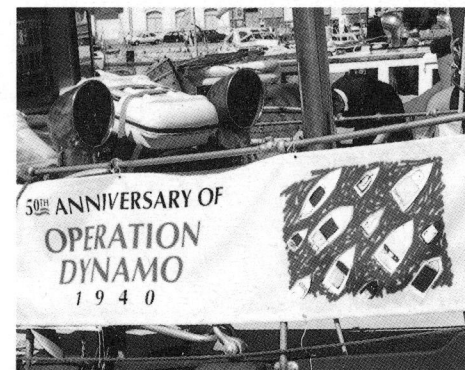

D The little ships return to Dunkirk

5 Why do you think these people continue to thank God for the way they were rescued?

JESUS' ATTITUDE

Jesus was concerned for the total well-being of the people he met. He wanted them to know about God and about spiritual values. He was also concerned with their physical well-being. He healed people and he was concerned when they were hungry.

One day when Jesus was preaching to several thousand people, he was worried that they were so far out into the desert that there would be nowhere for them to buy food. The **disciples** found a boy with a couple of bread rolls and some small sardines. Jesus used these to provide food for everyone in the vast crowd. Later on, when he was talking to the people, he told them that he himself was the 'Bread of Life'. Read the story for yourself in John:6.

When Jesus gave his disciples a symbol, or sign, of his presence, he used the ordinary things of life. Bread was the symbol he chose to represent his body. He chose wine to represent his blood. Every time people ate or drank these, they were to remember him. (I Corinthians:11) Food and drink therefore, are a sign of the presence of Christ. In offering food and drink to the hungry, Christians can be seen as offering them Christ himself.

CHRISTIAN ATTITUDES

The Early Church tried to make sure that everyone had sufficient food for their own needs. They shared equally, taking care that no one went hungry. Their object was to 'do good to all men, and especially to those who belong to the household of faith.' This meant that they regarded all believers in Jesus as members of the same family.

One of the problems was that the **apostles** found they were spending so much time organizing the sharing of food that they had little time to tell people the rest of Jesus' message. They didn't stop the food distribution . . . they simply

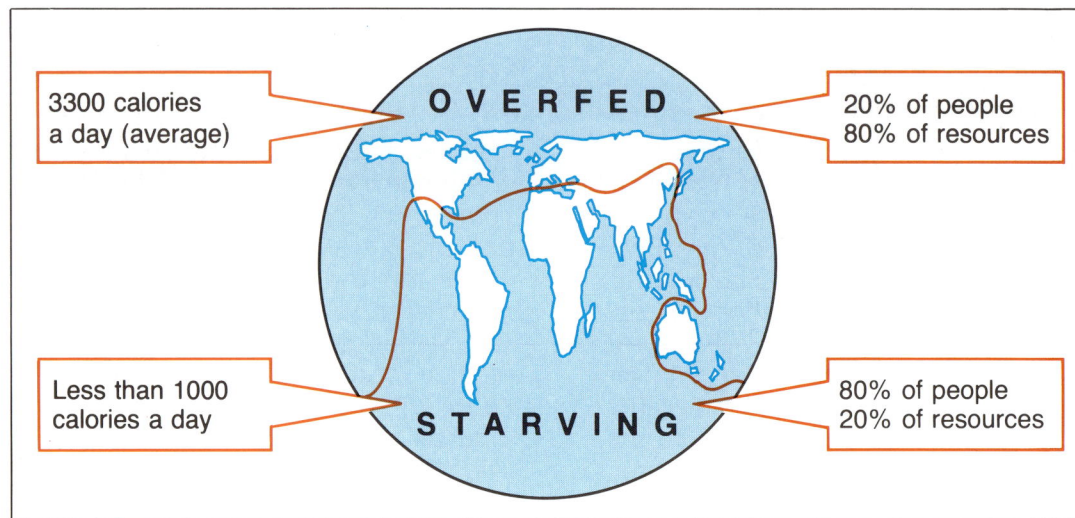

3300 calories a day (average)

OVERFED

20% of people
80% of resources

Less than 1000 calories a day

STARVING

80% of people
20% of resources

found other people to do it. It was a necessary part of their being Christian. (Acts 6:1–7)

Later, James made it quite clear that Christians had a responsibility to look after the poor and to make sure they had food and clothing. Faith, said James, was totally worthless without also caring about other people. (James 2:14–17)

Jesus taught that the attitude to wealth and poverty is what is important. There is nothing wrong with ownership. It is the failure to share which divides people both from their fellow people and from God. (Read the story of the rich man and Lazarus in Luke 16.)

REASONS FOR FOOD SHORTAGE

1 Lack of knowledge of how to produce sufficient nutritious food.

2 War, which prevents both the growing and distribution of food.

3 Political decisions by own and other governments.

4 Economic decisions by own and other governments, and by internal and external traders and manufacturers.

5 Human greed and selfishness, including growth of agribusiness, i.e. rich northern nations use poorer southern nations as market gardens to produce goods for northern supermarkets at prices the people in the north want to pay.

6 Famines: the failure to grow sufficient crops because of lack of rain or some other event beyond human control.

GIVE US THIS DAY OUR DAILY BREAD

When Jesus taught people to pray, he taught them to say, 'Give us this day our daily bread.' He didn't suggest saying *my* daily bread. Each Christian is praying for daily food as part of the world-wide family of Christians. It should be impossible for a Christian in a rich northern nation to pray for daily bread without also being prepared to do everything in their power to make sure that brothers and sisters in the poorer southern nations are also fed.

CHRISTIAN AID

It is this attitude which encouraged the **British Council of Churches** to set up Christian Aid in 1944. Income for this is provided by support groups throughout the UK, as well as the annual Christian Aid Week.

Christian Aid helps by supplying food for people who are undernourished and suffering from malnutrition. Sometimes this is in the form of direct aid, when there has been a famine or natural disaster. Later on it can take the form of providing seeds for next year's crops so that people can gain the self-respect of growing their own food. Christian Aid also provides health education and sends medical supplies and aid to disaster areas.

Much of Christian Aid's work involves educating people to understand the causes of poverty and injustice. Agricultural training is provided wherever possible and self-help schemes are promoted as a way of helping local populations to become self-supporting through the use of locally available natural resources.

CAFOD

In 1962 CAFOD, the Catholic Fund for Overseas Development, was started. This organization works very closely with Christian Aid in bringing practical aid to the world's poor. Like other Christian agencies working in poverty areas, CAFOD attempts to supply the basic needs of food and water, as well as tackling the problems of education, health, housing and work.

Most charities which try to help poor and hungry people would agree that what each one of them does is a drop in the ocean. However, they would also point to the fact that Jesus himself did not solve all the world's problems. He tackled those he met on a day to day basis. Christians are called to do the same.

NOTES/DATABASE

Look up the following words in the glossary. Then use the definition to make suitable entries for your notebook or database.

Disciples   Apostle
British Council of Churches

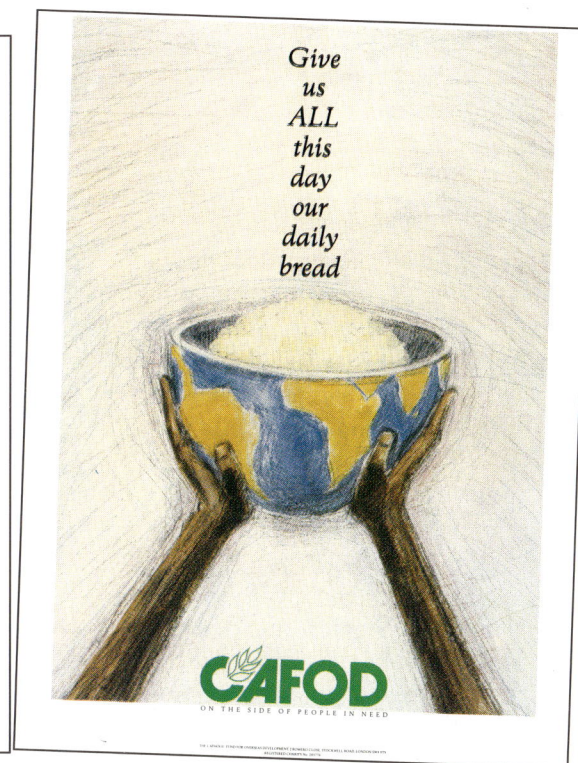

A and B Christian Aid and CAFOD: bringing practical aid to the world's poor

ACTIVITIES

1 **Quick quiz**

a In which ways was Jesus concerned about people?

b How did Jesus show his concern for people when he was preaching in the desert?

c What do you think he meant by calling himself the 'Bread of Life'?

d What signs did Jesus use to help people remember him?

e What did the Early Church do to show that the Christians were all one family?

f What problem did the apostles meet?

g How did they solve this problem?

h What was James' attitude to poor and hungry people?

i What was one thing which Jesus taught people to say when they prayed?

j How should Christians who have enough food react to this prayer?

k What is Christian Aid?

l In what ways does Christian Aid help people?

m How does Christian Aid educate people in Britain?

n What is CAFOD?

o What is CAFOD's aim?

p Do you think there is any point in doing a little to help when the problem is so enormous? Write down some reasons for your answer.

IT'S TOO LITTLE!

Many people say that the problems of feeding the poor people of the world are so great that there is little point in any of us trying to do anything as individuals. They regard it as the task of governments to help these people.

1 Read this story carefully

'Jesus sat down opposite the place where the offerings were put and watched the crowd putting their offerings into the temple treasury. Many rich people threw in large amounts. But a poor widow came, and put in two very small copper coins worth only a fraction of a penny. Calling his disciples to him, Jesus said, I tell you the truth, this poor widow has put more in than all the others.'
(Mark 12:41–43)

a What do you think Jesus meant by saying, 'She has given more than all the others'?

b Was there any point in giving so little? Write down some reasons for your answer.

2 **Discuss**

When someone gives something to a charity, is the person who receives the money (or food etc.) the only person who benefits?

FURTHER ACTIVITIES

THE RICH MAN AND LAZARUS

This story is in Luke 16:19–31.

There was once a rich man . . . who lived in luxury. There was also a poor man called Lazarus who was taken each day to the rich man's gate to eat table scraps. He was covered in sores.

The poor man died and went to heaven.

The rich man died and went to hell. When the rich man realized how awful the pains of hell were he wanted someone to go back and warn his brothers.

3 a What does this story tell us about people's attitude to the things which they own?

b What ought the rich man to have done during his lifetime?

c This story would make an excellent play. Read it carefully as well as looking at the cartoon version of it on this page. Now write your own play which explains this story clearly.

THE SHEEP AND THE GOATS

4 Read Matthew 25:31–46. This is a parable. A parable is a story with a hidden meaning. Look carefully for the hidden meaning.

a Who do you think the king is in this parable?

b How does the king decide who is going to belong in his kingdom?

c Did the people know that they were doing something for the king?

d Do you think that the king chooses people for his kingdom because of what they *believe* or because of what they *do*? Write down some reasons for your answer.

e Did the king exclude people from his kingdom, or did they exclude themselves? Write down some reasons for your answer.

5 **Discuss**

Is the Kingdom of God (according to Matthew 25 and your own opinions) just for Christians, or is it for people of all religions, or does it not matter whether you believe in God or not?

A 'Spaceship Earth'

'On Spaceship Earth, success is not about production and consumption, but about the nature, quality and length of life . . . If the Earth's resources are used wisely, they will continue to provide for both the material and spiritual needs of all mankind.'
(David Bellamy)

Food and water are our most basic human needs. They are also our most basic human rights.

Is there enough food? The answer is certainly that there is enough food to feed the world if it is managed properly.

B Mass food production

The world's cereal crop is sufficient to give everyone in the world 1 kilogram of grain a day. This is about 3000 **calories**, which is more than enough for healthy living. Increases in the number of people in the world are matched by the increases in food production. There has been an increase of 10 per cent in the last ten years.

Wealthy people are rarely killed by drought. It is always the poor who suffer. For example, in Asia, food production has increased but the poor people have become even poorer. This is because lack of food is just one of the differences between rich and poor.

Not all of the food produced feeds people. Cattle in the rich countries eat more than all the people in the poorer countries put together. Some food is wasted. There are various reasons for this.

Sometimes the prices would go too low if the food were sold. Economic factors govern its destruction.

Sometimes it joins a mountain of food which the **European Community** has amassed because of its Common Agricultural Policy. These mountains

C Some countries cannot grow enough food to support themselves

occur because governments and the European Community step in to buy surpluses when farmers have produced too much. Recently, there have been attempts to encourage farmers *not* to grow food because they are producing too much for local needs.

Why are surpluses not sent to poor countries where they need food? The usual answer is that it is too expensive to send it to these countries. Sometimes the food which is surplus to the needs of people in Europe is not suitable to be sent to countries where there is famine. This includes **commodities** like butter.

THE POOR SUFFER

Poor people suffer, particularly in **developing countries** in the continents of Africa, Asia and South America. They go hungry because they have no land of their own on which they can grow food. Often they are slum dwellers or live in shanty towns. Women and children are the people most at risk.

About 10 per cent of the world's population are seriously undernourished. In Africa one person in every six is in danger of dying of severe **malnutrition**.

Very often people are hungry because governments favour the better off. It is easier for large farmers to get loans to buy next year's seeds, than for small farmers. However, small farms are generally more productive than large farms. In Latin America, the small farms can produce as much as 14 times more per acre than the large farms.

WHO OWNS THE LAND?

A 1988 United Nations survey of 83 nations showed that 80 per cent of farmland was controlled by just 3 per cent of landowners.

Eighty per cent of the rural labour forces in Jamaica, Bolivia, the Philippines, Bangladesh and India have little or no land themselves on which to produce food.

Who eats the food from Third World farmland? The rich nations of Europe, America and Australasia (Australia and New Zealand) eat the produce of more than half the land in the Third World. Small farmers often get better prices by exporting the food they grow to the richer northern nations so they produce the kinds of foods which people in these countries want. These are usually luxuries which do not supply the basic food needs of the local population. Often the very people who are growing food for Europe and America are going hungry themselves.

It is a disturbing fact that large food production businesses from the rich countries use land in the poorer countries as a market garden. This is to satisfy the luxury requirements of the rich nations and to make a great deal of money for the businesses.

HOW SHOULD CHRISTIANS REACT?

'We cannot escape from the fact that (in Jesus' parable of the rich man and Lazarus) we are the rich man, clothed and fed in comfort, and also guilty of appalling negligence concerning the starving man at our gate. Since all that we are and all that we possess belong to God, we must one day give account of our stewardship to him.'
(Rev. David Watson in the foreword to *Rich Christians in an age of hunger* by Ronald Sider)

NOTES/DATABASE

Look up the following words in the glossary. Then use the definitions to make suitable entries for your notebook or database.

Calories
European Community
Commodities
Developing countries
Malnutrition

ACTIVITIES

1 Quick quiz

a What did David Bellamy call our planet?

b What are our most basic human rights?

c What do we need to do if there is to be enough food to feed the world?

d Who suffers most when there is a drought in a developing country?

e What happens to much of the world's cereal crop?

f Why is so much food wasted?

g Why are food surpluses not sent to countries where extra food is needed?

h Who suffers most from lack of food?

i How many people in Africa are severely undernourished?

j Write down one example of the way governments favour richer people.

k Who eats most of the food produced by the poorer countries?

l Why might someone who is growing food for sale in Europe or America be going hungry themselves?

m How do some large businesses from the northern nations make use of land in the poorer southern nations?

2 How should Christians respond?

Look at the chart which lists some of the ways in which the world can begin to respond to the problem of unequal distribution of food. Using the information there, as well as your own ideas, write an article for a school newspaper called 'Distributing the food fairly'.

World-scale help	Individual help
Land and resources should be shared more equally.	Learn more about the causes of world hunger.
Small farmers need more help with borrowing money, getting water, and obtaining technical help and fair prices.	Think about what we eat and where it was produced.
Families need more advice on nutrition and growing crops.	Write to our MP and Euro MP.
People who are very poor, and own no land, need help in getting work.	Tell everyone we know – in school, at church, in youth groups and our own families about poorer countries.
Developing countries need better prices for their exports.	Support Christian and other organisations like Tear Fund and Traidcraft, which are trying to help.

FURTHER ACTIVITIES

A POUND OF BANANAS

Where the money goes when you pay £1 for bananas

1 **Discuss**

Do you think it is right that the person who sells the bananas gets nearly three times as much as the people who grow and pick them?

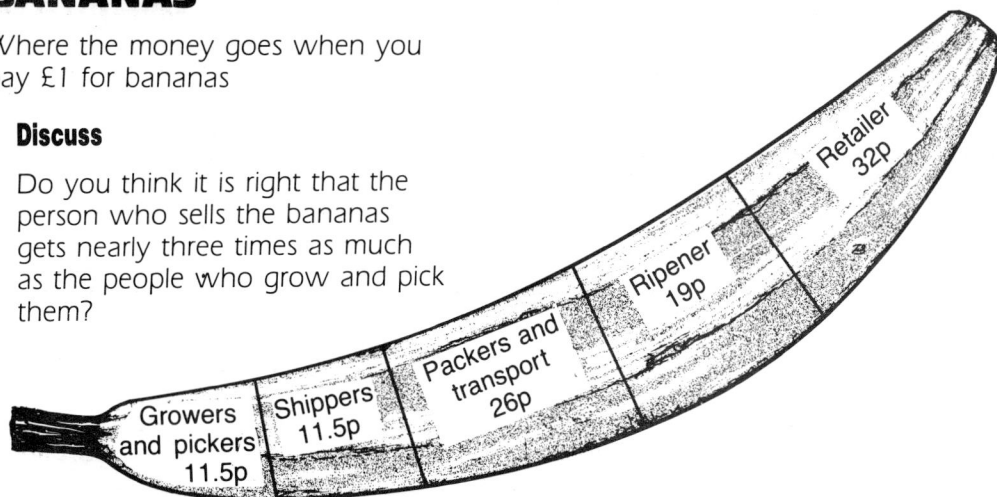

Retailer 32p

Ripener 19p

Packers and transport 26p

Shippers 11.5p

Growers and pickers 11.5p

D How are Traidcraft plantations different from others?

Alternative trading organizations such as Traidcraft are working towards giving a fairer proportion of money to the people who actually produce the food and commodities in developing countries. Like Tear Fund, Traidcraft is a Christian organization. They have set up coffee and tea plantations which pay fair wages. The workers are given a good working environment. The organizations are also involved in self-help schemes. This generally involves the setting up of local co-operatives which produce local crafts, goods and commodities. The goods are then marketed for the local people in the West at a fair price. Sometimes western experts are sent to help local people design goods based on traditional crafts and local materials. These can be guaranteed a ready market in the West. Like other Christian organizations, Tear Fund and Traidcraft are interested in the welfare of every individual in a community. Sponsorship and community schemes attempt to improve standards of health care as well as living standards.

2 Find out as much as you can about Traidcraft. Their address is: Kingsway, Gateshead, Tyne and Wear NE11 0NE.

You might like to invite a local representative of Traidcraft to come and tell you about their work. They have a large fashion collection. It might be possible to plan a fashion show in which you model the clothes made in the poorer countries. This would give you the opportunity to tell many people about the needs of poorer countries.

NORTH/SOUTH MAP

Look at the North/South map.

North/South is a convenient way of dividing the world into rich and poor countries. Above the line (northern countries plus Australasia) are the richer countries. These include Europe, North America, USSR, Japan and Australasia.

The poorer countries in the South are often called Third World or developing countries.

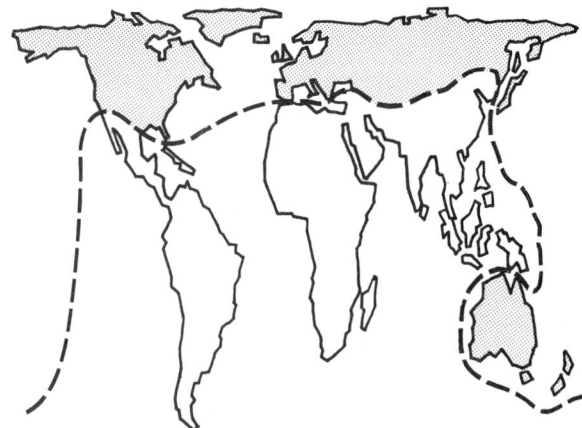

3 Look at the chart on the right.

a Which country has the largest population?

b Copy the North/South map on the left-hand page, using a colour to show the countries of the developing world.

c Using the statistics in the chart write down some reasons why you think that Bangladesh needs to receive the largest amount of food aid.

d Why do you think that the people in Chad have one of the lowest life expectancies in the world?

Country	Population (millions)	Area (thousands of sq. kms)	Population density	GNP per person (dollars)	Food aid in cereals (thousand of metric tons)	Life expectancy
Bangladesh	103·2	144	716·7	160	1287	50
Burkina Faso	8·1	274	29·6	150	109	47
Chad	5·1	1284	4·0	–	74	45
Ethiopia	43·5	1222	35·6	120	793	46
Kenya	21·2	583	36·4	300	139	57
Malawi	7·4	119	62·2	160	5	45
Mali	7·6	1240	6·1	180	83	47
Mozambique	14·2	802	17·7	210	252	48
Nepal	17·0	141	120·6	150	9	47
Sudan	22·6	2506	9·1	320	904	49
Uganda	15·2	236	64·4	230	7	48
United Kingdom	56·7	245	231·4	8870	–	75

4 Look at the chart on the right.

a Which country receives
(i) the most aid per person?
(ii) the least aid per person?

b (i) One dollar equals approximately 60 pence. Calculate how much money Bangladesh receives in aid per person per year. Write down your answer in pounds and pence.

(ii) Using the amount of money you have calculated above, go to your local supermarket and work out what food you could purchase for this amount of money. Make sure you select food which would produce a balanced diet.

If you have a suitable spread sheet program on your computer, use it to calculate and display the results.

(iii) Work out how many days this would last you. Remember, this is the amount of food aid for a *year* in Bangladesh.

Official development assistance per person 1986 (in dollars)

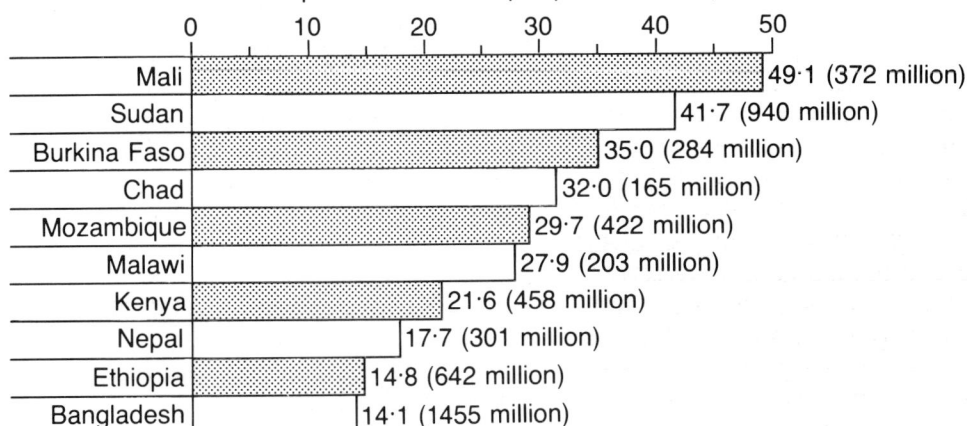

Mali	49·1 (372 million)
Sudan	41·7 (940 million)
Burkina Faso	35·0 (284 million)
Chad	32·0 (165 million)
Mozambique	29·7 (422 million)
Malawi	27·9 (203 million)
Kenya	21·6 (458 million)
Nepal	17·7 (301 million)
Ethiopia	14·8 (642 million)
Bangladesh	14·1 (1455 million)

Figures in brackets give the total amount received by that country.

Sources: World Development Report, 1988

5 Read I Corinthians 16:1-4.

Paul raised money to help people during a famine. Look at the way in which Paul tells Christians to collect the money. Do you think this is an appropriate way for Christians to work out how much money they should give?

In the Bible, water and rain are regarded as a special sign of God's blessing. This is not surprising, as the Bible has its origins in Israel, a land where there are very few rivers. In most parts of Israel there is little rainfall. Galilee is the only really fertile area. Many parts of the land are covered by semi-desert.

Water is vital for life. Two-thirds of a person's body weight is made up of water. No one can live more than a few days without water.

Three quarters of the earth's surface is covered in water but less than 1 per cent of this is the fresh water which people need to stay alive.

WHO USES THE WATER?

The richer, northern nations have greater rainfall. This means that they also have more fresh-water rivers and lakes as well as large reservoirs. They therefore have access to greater supplies of usable water.

Water is used in homes for a large

A Collecting water, in Africa . . .

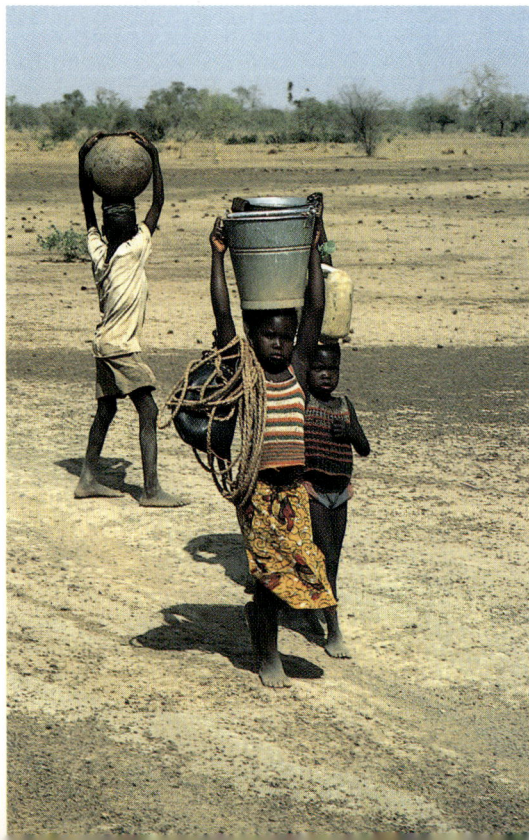

range of purposes but the largest user of water in the richer nations is industry.

Rainfall is less in the southern nations. Only the rich can afford the luxury of piped water in their homes. Villages in many parts of Africa are lucky if they have a stand pipe and village wells can often become contaminated. Water supplies are often several miles away from someone's home.

Water is a necessity for life but for many people it is a luxury which must be carefully rationed. Without adequate water for irrigating crops, dry farming methods can produce very little. This puts the small farmer who cannot afford to dig wells or irrigate his land at a disadvantage. The richer agribusinesses can afford the water, so they take what they need. Their crops often go to feed people in the North, where prices are higher.

ACCCESS TO WATER

In developing countries, three out of five people do not have easy access to clean water. They may have to walk for hours to collect a few litres of it. It is usually the women who have to do this job. Women also make up the majority of farmers in poorer countries. When they are working in the fields or fetching water, women often have to carry small children with them.

Much of the water available to people in poorer countries is, by European standards, unsafe to drink. It is frequently a severe health hazard.

B . . . in Thailand . . .

SOME REASONS FOR LACK OF WATER SUPPLIES

There is sometimes underground water in the poorer countries. To reach it drilling equipment and expertise are needed. These skills are not usually available to poor people. Hand-dug wells are the traditional wells of the villages, and these can't always be dug deep enough to reach reserves of water. Poor sanitation and pollution has made many of the rivers in the developing world unsafe to be used as drinking water.

In Brazil, it is not unusual for rural families to be forced off the land because rich people have fenced off the water without any legal right to do so. This has meant that people have had nowhere to water their cattle and so have had to move on in search of water. Caste divisions (the family people belong to) in India have stopped some people using the water which is used by families of a higher caste.

There have sometimes been problems when new wells have been dug. In West Africa, the fresh water from deep tube-wells tastes unfamiliar and people have been afraid to use it.

CONTAMINATED WATER

Water can be polluted by poor sanitation, by dead animals in the water, by some types of plant life, and by some small creatures which inhabit water. There are great dangers in drinking

C . . . and in a refugee camp in Hong Kong

contaminated water. A very large proportion of all illnesses are water related. In developing countries 10 million people a year die from diarrhoea caused by drinking contaminated water. Some diseases are spread by insects which

breed in the water. Others are carried by worms which spend part of their lives in the water. At least 200 million people in 70 countries have Bilharzia, a water-carried disease which robs people of strength and energy.

CHRISTIAN RESPONSIBILITY

Jesus said that he was 'living water' and that anyone who believed in him would never be thirsty again. Christians know that Jesus was talking in picture language about spiritual thirst. They cannot, however, ignore the need to provide water for their brothers and sisters in parts of the world where lack of water means poor health or even death.

ACTIVITIES

1 **Quick quiz**

a Why is water regarded as a sign of God's blessing in the Bible?

b How long can a person live without water?

c Why do the richer northern countries have greater reserves of water?

d How is most of the water used in the richer northern countries?

e Why is there less water in reserve in the southern countries?

f Who are the only people to have water in their homes in the poorer countries?

g Where do poorer people get their water?

h In what ways is the small farmer disadvantaged in areas where there is little water?

i In developing countries, how many people do not have access to clean water?

j How do people get their water if there is none in their own village?

k Make a list of the reasons why water is often not available in developing countries.

l What dangers are there in using polluted water?

INVESTIGATE YOUR WATER SUPPLY

2 a Do you know where your water comes from? Most of you will be able to turn on a tap and expect clean, fresh water to come gushing out. But how did it arrive in your tap? Write to your local water authority. Ask them how the water got to the tap. Is it from a reservoir, an underground river or some other source?

b When you have found out where the water comes from, draw a map or diagram of its route to you. If you have a CAD package for your computer, you could use it to draw the map or diagram.

c You might like to write an article for the school newspaper explaining how the water gets to your area.

D These Inuit Alaskans melt snow for water

3 Where do other people get their water?

a Now you know where your water comes from try and contact a school in a different part of the world to find out how they get their water. If your school has a computer linked by modem to a bulletin board or to a network such as Campus 2000, it should be possible to receive answers from several different areas of the world. Missionary societies will also put you in touch with schools in other parts of the world.

b When you have received the information, use it to make a display which will help to inform other people about the needs for clean water in other parts of the world.

4 What reasons can you think of for European and American Christians trying to help developing countries to get adequate water supplies?

CHOLERA HITS THE CAMPS

An outbreak of cholera was reported amongst Vietnamese 'boat people' in detention centres in Hong Kong. The outbreak affects 'boat people' housed on the Soko Islands, one of the most inhospitable sites being used to accommodate 'boat people'. The islands were evacuated in July because of Typhoon Gordon. At the time, Phillip Barker, Save the Children's field director in Hong Kong, warned against the re-use of the islands because of the health risk caused by lack of basic sanitation and fresh water.

As far as we are aware, this is the first time that cholera has hit 'boat people'. But, with the increasing use of extreme sites such as the Soko Islands, the threat of serious disease has been increasingly likely, said Phillip Barker. Recent surveys have shown that the 'boat people' are receiving barely a third of the minimum amount of fresh water that is required for basic needs. Save the Children is particularly concerned about the dangers of disease spreading. A recent Save the Children survey found that 30% of the 'boat people' were close to malnutrition and, there-fore, in a very weak condition to fight off disease.

The Director General wrote to 'The Times' outlining the Fund's view that any arrangements for the future of the boat people must include an improvement in their present living conditions; acceleration of screening and resettlement/repatriation procedures; adequate support and protection for those resettled or repatriated; and renewed development aid to Vietnam.

As conditions in many camps worsen, SCF has agreed to take over health and education services for under-fives in three more camps for new arrivals.

1 **Read the report carefully.**

Now answer these questions:

a Which disease has broken out among the boat people?

b What are the main health risks in the Soko islands?

c How much fresh water are the boat people receiving?

d How has the Save the Chidren Fund agreed to help?

e Why do you think that many Christians who want to help children in other countries choose to give money to the Save the Children Fund?

EPCOT CENTER, WALT DISNEY WORLD, ORLANDO, FLORIDA

Scientists who work in the Land Pavilion at the Epcot Center are co-operating with scientists at the Kennedy Space Center, Cape Canaveral, in a number of agricultural experiments. Some of these involve growing plants on rotating arms with the roots at the top, and no soil. Other methods include mixed farming where plants are grown in rows of tall and short plants which need different environments.

Trickle watering of plants is one of the most interesting experiments. This involves the computer control of irrigation which supplies the exact number of drops of water which a plant needs to grow. It is supplied directly to the roots of the plant which avoids the wastage of precious water. These methods of farming could be of use in desert farming where there is little water available, as well as in potential colonies in space.

2 **Discuss**

Why do you think that scientists at the Epcot Center, Disney World, are co-operating with the Kennedy Space Center to experiment with methods of farming?

WATER IN THE BIBLE

In Biblical times water was precious in Israel as there were very few rivers. Rainfall was also low. Water was collected by families in their own cisterns, but this was rarely 'sweet water', good for drinking. Wells which had good water became popular spots both for local people and travellers.

Rain was regarded in the Bible as a special sign of God's blessing. (Joel 2:23)

Jesus once met a women by the Jacob's well in Samaria. Look at John 4 to find out about his conversation with her.

E A traditional water pump in Egypt

4 Read carefully Joel 2:23–27.

Now answer these questions:

a Who is asked to rejoice?

b What has God given them?

c What are the results of this?

This is intended as an example to show the people of Israel that God goes on loving and caring for his people.

5 Something to think about

If you lived in a country where there was very little rainfall, how would you react to rain?
    Why do you think that the people who wrote the Bible thought of rain as a sign of God's blessing?

6 Water and life
Isaiah 55:1–2, John 6:37–39.

Remember, water is essential for life and Jesus said that the Holy Spirit was essential for Christian life.
    Look up these two references then answer the questions below.

a Why do you think Jesus has quoted Isaiah?

b What does Jesus add?

c Why do you think Jesus links the gift of water with the gift of the Holy Spirit?

3 Use John 4:13–15 to fill in the speech bubbles for the rest of the conversation between Jesus and the woman.

Are you greater than our father Abraham who gave us this well?

7 Research project
Use a concordance to look up the references to 'water' and 'rain' in the Bible. Now write a short article about the meaning of water in the Bible.

'A *healthy* person is one who is free from physical, mental and spiritual illness.'
(Christian Aid)

'Everyone has a right . . . to medical care.'
(UN Declaration on Human Rights)

POOR PEOPLE ARE THE MOST LIKELY TO BE ILL

Some people in the world today are more likely to be ill than others. These are the very poor people who live in the developing countries. Many of these countries are located in Asia, Africa and South America.

Poor people in these countries often do not have access to clean water. Frequently, they do not have enough of the right foods to eat. They sometimes

A Malnutrition causes millions of deaths each year

live in conditions with little or no sanitation. They rarely have easy access to medical care.

Lack of body building foods is a frequent cause of illness. At least one in nine people in the world is severely undernourished. The Food and Agricultural Organization (FAO), which is part of the United Nations, says that over 40 million people each year die from severe malnutrition.

CHRISTIAN INVOLVEMENT IN HEALTH CARE

When Jesus was asked whether or not he was the Messiah he told people to look around them and see what was happening. He said, 'The blind can see, the lame can walk, those who suffer from dreaded skin diseases are made clean, the deaf can hear, and the Good News is preached to the poor.' Healing people, making people whole in every way, was at the heart of Jesus' message.

Christians have always been involved in healing. Missionary societies in the 19th and early 20th centuries were often the only source of organized health care in some parts of the world. Christian organizations are still involved in health care, particularly in areas where there is very little. Many Christians are involved in the medical and caring professions, which is how they work out their vocation.

CHILDREN SUFFER MOST

About two-thirds of the world's under fives do not get enough body building foods. At least 15 million children die of hunger every year. Some children are already weak and have less resistance to diseases because they do not have enough of the right food.

There are many diseases which can easily be cured in the rich countries but which kill people in poorer countries. For example, there are at least 100 million

under fives in the developing countries who suffer permanently from diarrhoea. Every year, over 6 million of them die from diarrhoea.

Five million children in developing countries die each year from measles, whooping cough, polio, tetanus, diphtheria and tuberculosis.

CAUSES OF DISEASE

Some diseases are caused by lack of food. Here are a few examples.

Kwashiokor is caused by lack of protein in the diet. It is especially common among young children.

Marasmus is a more serious form of kwashiokor. This damages both physical and mental growth.

Anaemia is caused by a lack of iron in the diet. This leads to a lack of energy as well as a loss of appetite.

Some diseases are related to the lack of clean water. These include:

Diarrhoea, which leads to dehydration and loss of weight. It is caused by drinking and using contaminated water.

B Diseases caused by polluted water.

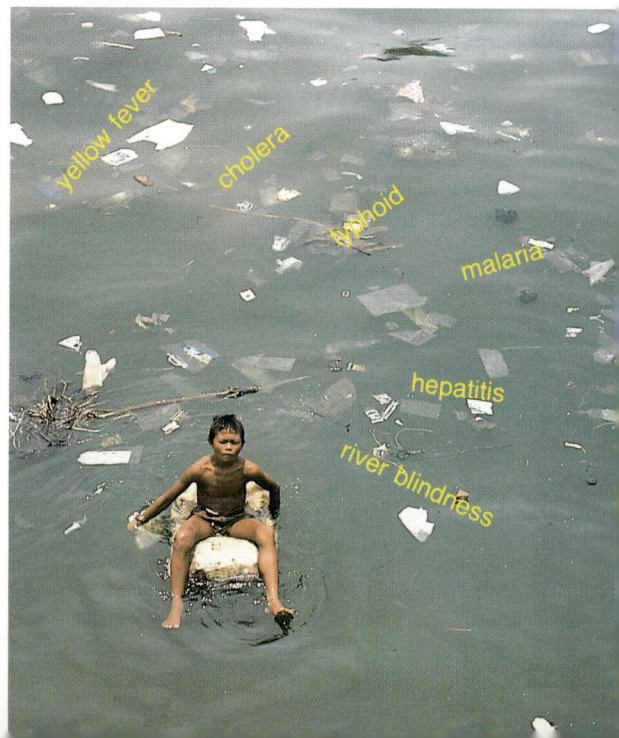

Bilharzia, an infection in the blood stream caused by tiny organisms carried by snails which live in water. The organisms pass into human beings through the mouth and skin.

In rich countries, most people have a reasonable standard of living. Even there, it is the poor people who are more likely to become ill because they are sometimes undernourished, and often poorly housed.

Primary health care

Estimates from the World Health Organisation suggest that three-quarters of the world's diseases could be prevented through the provision of primary health care. This would provide basic health care in local communities.

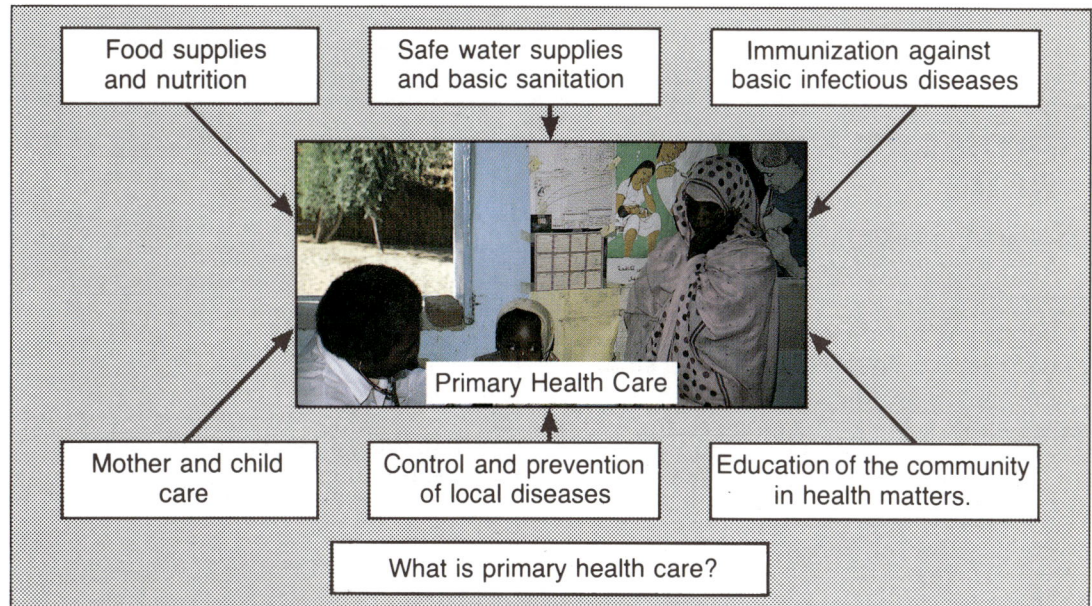

Food supplies and nutrition

Safe water supplies and basic sanitation

Immunization against basic infectious diseases

Primary Health Care

Mother and child care

Control and prevention of local diseases

Education of the community in health matters.

What is primary health care?

ACTIVITIES

1 Quick quiz

a What is a healthy person?

b Where do the people live who are most likely to be ill?

c Make a list of some of the reasons why poor people become ill.

d How many people in the world die each year from severe malnutrition?

e What did Jesus say in answer to the question 'Are you the Messiah?'

f Why are Christians often involved in the medical professions?

g Why do so many children have little resistance to diseases?

h Why do you think that diseases which can be cured easily in the rich countries can kill people who live in the poorer countries?

i Make a list of some of the diseases which are caused by lack of food.

j Which diseases are caused by lack of clean water?

k Why does poor housing often lead to disease?

l How does the World Health Organization (WHO) think that 85 per cent of the world's diseases could be prevented?

C This scene in Indonesia reveals many health risks

FURTHER ACTIVITIES

PRIMARY HEALTH CARE

'Nothing makes me scream more than people calling primary health care primitive medicine for primitive people. What they are really saying is: "Let's continue to give good hospital based medical care to 5–10 per cent of the population – and let that siphon off 80–90 per cent of the health budget!"'
(Dr Halfdan Mahler, Director General, World Health Organization)

1 Discuss

Christians see giving money to help human need as part of being a Christian. Why do you think a Christian might choose to give money to help provide primary health care?

Small Ads
Under £10

Bargain Price: Immunize a child against 6 diseases. Only £2.60 for each child.

Primary Health Care: Look after a person's basic health care for only £9 per year.

Clean Water for all: Eliminate some diseases by providing clean water for everyone. Under £10 per person.

2 Discuss

How could primary health care help the boat people who live in the camp described in the article in Unit 21 (see page 86)?

3 Help people to understand what primary health care is all about.

Many people might wish to help provide primary health care for developing countries if they knew a little more about it. Look at the information in this unit to help you plan an advertising campaign to tell people about primary health care.

You will need to design posters and leaflets which help to get the message across. Make sure that your large billboard designs do not have too much information on them. People need to get the message quickly as they drive past.

The World Health Organisation (WHO)	The United Nations International Children's Emergency Fund (UNICEF)
Set up in 1948 Aims to protect and promote world health Helps to: a) set up health programmes; b) monitor disease on a world scale; c) make sure drugs are made safely; d) share information about medical matters around the world; e) provide money to try to help get rid of diseases.	Provides care for mothers and children WHO and UNICEF both provide Primary Health Care, training local people to give basic health care in the community. Charities like Christian Aid and CAFOD help to provide the money for this kind of work.

4 Look at the drawings below

Imagine you live in a village about 100 miles from the hospital. You have no motor transport, and no cash. You are already weak because you are unable to eat the right foods. You have broken your leg.

a How do you think you could get to the hospital?

b What form of transport do you think you could use?

c How long do you think it would take to get to the hospital?

d Do you think your family would take you there?

e What do you think the result of your accident would be?

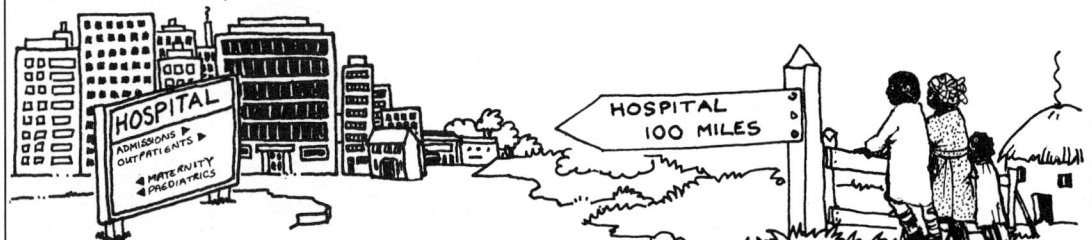

Hospitals in town centres provide care for serious illness, and specialist training. BUT

85% of people in developing countries live in rural areas

5 Look carefully at the table on the right.

a Which five countries have the lowest infant mortality rate?

b Why do you think there is such a contrast between the number of babies who die in these countries and the numbers who die in the countries in the developing world like Ethiopia?

c What do you think could be done to try to prevent so many deaths in the first year of life in poor countries?

Infant mortality rates for 1986. The figures are of the number of infants who die before the age of one, per thousand live births

Finland	6
Hong Kong	8
UK	9
USA	10
Sudan	108
Bangladesh	121
Nepal	130
Burkina Faso	140
Mali	144
Malawi	153
Ethiopia	155

Source: World Development Report 1988

8 Something to think about

Why do you think that the country with the highest infant mortality rate also has the lowest life expectancy?

9 Use a concordance of the Bible to look up 'health', 'heal', 'healing'.

a Make a list of some of the important references.

b Prepare a display which shows what the Bible says about health and healing.

c Why do you think that Jesus healed so many people?

JESUS' ATTITUDE TO HEALTH AND HEALING

Jesus wanted people to be whole in body, mind and spirit. It was just as important to him that a person should be at peace with himself and with God as that he should be physically well. On one occasion, he forgave a man's sins. As a sign that he had the power to forgive sins, Jesus went on to heal the man, who was also unable to walk. (Mark 2:1–12).

6 Look carefully at Mark 2:1–12.

a What was the first thing that Jesus said to the man?

b Why did the religious leaders complain about Jesus' words?

c What did Jesus tell the man to do?

d Why did Jesus do this?

7 Look at the chart below.

a Which country has the highest life expectancy?

b Which country has the lowest life expectancy?

c Make a list of methods which would raise the life expectancy in Ethiopia?

Life expectancy in various countries, 1986

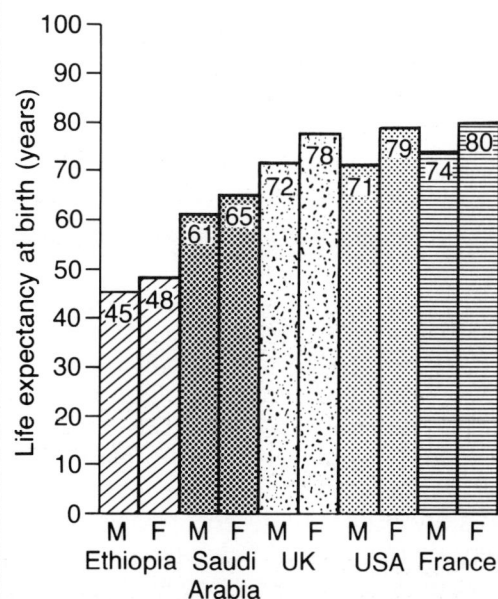

Source: World Development Report, 1988

10 Something to think about

Jesus did not heal everyone who was sick. For example, he may have seen the beggar, who was healed by Peter and John (Acts 3) many times, and *not* healed him. Why do you think Jesus healed some people, but not others?

11 Find out

Many Christians have been involved in healing of various kinds. Collect stories of Christians involved in this kind of work. You may find the *Faith in Action* series of booklets (RMEP) very helpful.

You might like to write to a missionary society to find out how some Christians are involved in medicine and healing as mission partners in various parts of the world today.

COMMUNICATIONS

Modern communications have made the world seem smaller. Telecommunications have allowed people all over the world to communicate with one another instantly. By telephone we can talk to people anywhere in the world, at comparatively little cost. Fax machines allow us to pass documents, including pictures, around the world easily. Electronic mail allows us to be linked by computer to people anywhere in the world. Television gives us an insight into what is happening in the world as soon as it happens. It also keeps us informed about some of the more important issues in the world today.

As people have begun to see the world beyond their immediate experience, they have also become more aware of some of its problems. Racial tension and the political changes in Eastern Europe, for example, cannot remain someone else's problem when they are shown on the screens of televisions in our own homes.

THE MEDIA HELP US CARE FOR OTHERS

The media, and in particular television, have helped us to understand the issues facing the world. They have shown us the plight of children – abandoned in Romania; facing certain death from malnutrition in Ethiopia; and caught up in war in the Lebanon. And people have responded. They have sent money to help and begun collections to raise larger sums of money. Some have hired transport and led mercy missions to help to alleviate the problems.

THE MEDIA SHOW US HOW WE ARE DAMAGING OUR PLANET

It is also largely through the media that we have come to see the damage we are doing to our planet. People are now

A Modern communications: a space satellite

aware, for example, of the 'greenhouse effect', the damage caused by acid rain, and the destruction of the rain forests. People no longer see these things as someone else's problem. We are more aware of our responsibility in all these matters. We know that we each need to play our part in the conservation of our planet.

THE BIBLICAL ATTITUDE

In the Bible, people were given the responsibility for looking after the world. In Genesis 1:26–30, Adam was given the task of looking after the animals of the world. Green plants were given to him for food, as were seed-bearing plants and fruit. His task was to rule the world. In this story, Adam represents people of every nation, and of every time. Their responsibility is still exactly the same as that which God gave to Adam in the Bible.

CHRISTIAN RESPONSIBILITY

This attitude of responsibility towards the world has been rediscovered as a central part of the Christian message. Christians accept that they are all brothers and sisters, 'children of the same heavenly Father'. To treat each other as brother or sister means sharing in each other's situation. This involves trying to share food resources, often by sending money to other parts of the world. It also means sharing in responsibility for natural resources. Christians call this 'stewardship'. It means understanding that everything on earth belongs to God, who created it. People hold the world in trust from God, with the responsibility of looking after it properly.

That is part of the reason why Christians have often been involved in environmental issues and projects. Traidcraft, a Christian alternative trading organization, has long been concerned with issues of conservation. It was one of the first groups actively involved in marketing recycled paper and has fought to re-introduce local crafts to areas of the developing world. Crafts in these areas had often been destroyed by Imperialist policies in the 19th and early 20th centuries.

Many Christians are also involved in groups which actively oppose the slaughter of animals for fur, as well as the slaughter of whales and other endangered species. This is one more area in which Christians and others have felt it right to stand up for their beliefs and to speak out against governments.

Christians see their faith as being more and more relevant in today's world. The standards which Jesus set, of loving and caring for everyone, have become even more important as people have become more aware of the inequalities in the world. Here is what Jesus would say in today's situation:

'I was hungry and you fed me, I was thirsty and you gave me a drink, I was a stranger and you received me into your homes, naked and you clothed me, in prison and you visited me.'

The righteous will then answer him, 'When, Lord, did we ever see you hungry and feed you, thirsty and give you a drink? When did we see you a stranger and welcome you into our homes, or naked and clothe you? When did we ever see you sick or in prison and visit you?'

Jesus replied, 'I tell you, whenever you did it for one of these least important of my brothers, you did it for me.'
(Matthew 25:34f)

ACTIVITIES

SOME OF THE WAYS THE WORLD IS ABUSED

1 Quick quiz

a Make a list of some of the modern methods of communication.

b How have people's attitudes changed as they have begun to see the world outside their own immediate experience?

c Why do you think people may react and respond more to world problems if they see them on television?

d How have the media helped people to become more aware of some of the problems facing the world?

e What are some of the environmental issues highlighted by television programmes?

f Which Biblical character was given the task of looking after the world?

g Why do Christians and others believe that this indicates that everyone has a responsibility to look after the world properly?

h What do Christians mean by stewardship?

i Why do you think that Christians have become involved in Alternative Trading Organizations.

j What other pressure groups are there which try to stand up for what they believe to be right?

gases puncturing the ozone layer

gases from burning fossil fuels

aviation fuel

leaks from nuclear installations

rocket debris

acid rain

acid rain

whaling

chemicals

poisonous waste
sewerage

oil slicks

lead compounds from car exhausts

over fishing

over cultivation

over use of pesticides and fertilisers

hunting for ivory, fur etc.

deforestation

over grazing

open cast mining

2 Draw your own version of the picture of the abuse of the world's resources. There may be other things which you would like to add to the picture.

FURTHER ACTIVITIES

B Famine in Ethiopia often features in the news

WHAT'S NEWS?

Watch an edition of the news on one of the television channels.

Here is a typical flow chart of a news broadcast. There may be a different number of stories in the edition you watched but the outline is probably similar.

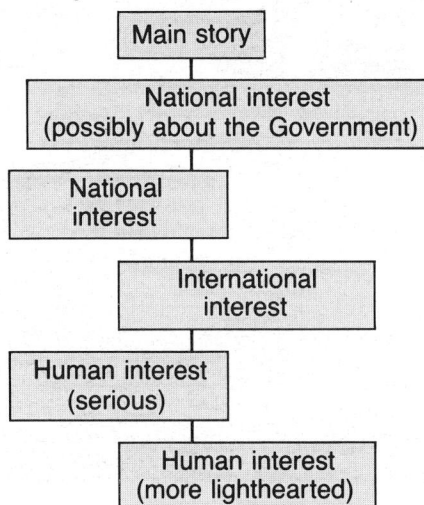

```
Main story
    │
National interest
(possibly about the Government)
    │
National
interest
    │
International
interest
    │
Human interest
(serious)
    │
Human interest
(more lighthearted)
```

1 a Design your own flow chart of the broadcast which you choose to watch.

b Do you think that watching this edition of the news helped you to understand your own country's responsibility in the world? Give reasons.

c How might a Christian use the news to help them to
(i) pray for the world
(ii) decide to give some money to charity?

2 Look through a list of the week's television programmes. Make a list of those which might draw people's attention to some world issues. Try to watch one of these programmes. Now use the information you gained from the programme to prepare a short talk on one issue which seems important in the world today.

3 The poster below advertises a competition to encourage young people's involvement in improving their environment.

Blue Peter
SAINSBURY'S
GREENSCHEME

Blue Peter and Sainsbury's have joined forces to help young people protect and improve their surroundings.

Have you an idea for something you would like to do to cheer up your area? If so, our GREENSCHEME could give you the money which, together with your hard work, will make it happen. It does not matter how big or how small the project is.

You might want to create a wildlife garden at school, or to clear out an old pond that's full of rubbish. You might need help setting up a recycling scheme, or you might want to clear graffiti from a wall in the town centre.

a Do you think it is a good idea to encourage young people in this way? Why?

b How might you contribute in a practical way to keeping your own school environment pleasant for everyone to live in?

c Design a project, based on a local area, which might be helpful to the environment. You will need to plan carefully. This will include costing the project, and making sure that it is something which you would be allowed to do. You may also need to draw plans. Perhaps you may need to approach the local council with an offer of dealing with a certain job, such as tidying up a footpath or clearing out a pond.

SATELLITE SYSTEM

Your school probably has its own weather station which may include a satellite system for displaying satellite weather broadcasts on a computer. The pictures you receive are usually based on transmissions from two geosynchronous satellites (moving at the same speed as the earth) which are located above Europe. These will give you up-to-date information about the weather. You will be able to produce your own weather forecasts.

4 These satellites also transmit 'false colour images' of the vegetation patterns over Europe. Start to collect this data. It will gradually help you see how the forestation patterns of Europe are changing. This has become a particular problem in Scotland and Scandinavia.

A warning! Don't expect quick results on this project. You will need to collect the data over a period of years to see any change.

Like most environmental projects, real change can only be seen over a long period. If you start to collect this information now, it could be of real use to people in your school in several years time. In the same way, if you plant more trees now, they could be of real use to the world in many years time.

C 'Respect nature'

WHAT THE BIBLE SAYS:

Man is in charge of the world's resources.
Genesis 1:27–30, Psalm 8:6–8

Be careful how you use the earth's resources.
Exodus 23:10–11

Don't damage trees, respect nature.
Deuteronomy 20:19,22–6

Share resources with those in need.
2 Corinthians 8:14–15

Share with all your neighbours, wherever in the world they may be.
Luke 10:27

5 Look at the Bible verses in the chart above. Use them to write an article called 'The Bible's attitude to world resources'.

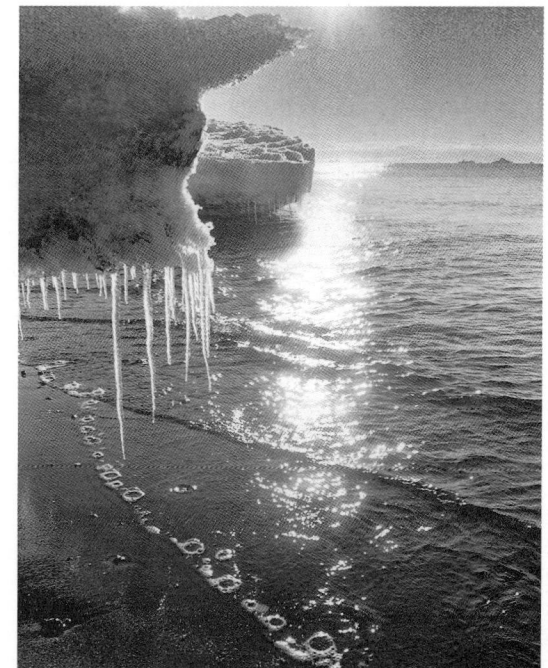

D An environment to be respected

Agribusiness   Large companies involved in farming on a massive scale

Apostle   Someone sent out with a special message

Birth certificate   The certificate issued when the birth of a baby is registered

Boycott   A refusal to use goods or services to achieve a political end

British Council of Churches   Organization of most Churches in the United Kingdom

Calories   A unit to describe the energy value of food

Child benefit   A sum of money paid weekly to mothers in the UK

Christians   People who believe that Jesus of Nazareth was sent by God to show the world how God wanted people to live

Church   A group of people who meet together to worship Jesus. A building in which Christians gather together to worship

Citizen   A person belonging to a nation who has both rights and responsibilities within that nation

Clergy   Ordained church leaders

Commodities   Goods such as tea, coffee, sugar, etc.

Communist regime   Government imposed by the Communist Party

Community   A group of people living near one another in a sociable way

Covenant   An agreement between people and groups

Creation   The act of God by which the universe came into being

Developing countries   Poor countries, known as the Third World

Disciple   A person who follows and learns from someone else

Discrimination   Making decisions unfairly based on colour, race, political belief, gender, etc.

Employment   Paid work

Endangered species   Animals which are threatened with extinction

European Community (EC)   An economic group of European countries

Evangelical   A Christian who believes strongly in Biblical truth expressed in practical action

Famine   Lack of food crops, often due to drought

Handfasting   An old ceremony in Scotland and Scandinavia when people agreed to live together before being married

Immigrants   People who have chosen to live in a country other than their own

Jesus   A man who lived in Israel in the time of the Romans, who Christians believe to be the son of God

Jewish faith   A belief in one God who is revealed in the Old Testament and who leads and guides his people, the Jews

Judaism   The belief of the Jews

Kingdom of Heaven   The perfect rule of God within the lives of people

Last Supper   The last meal which Jesus had with his disciples on the night before he died.

Leisure   A time when people can choose what they do

Liberation Theology   Originally a South American movement of Catholic priests who believe it right to engage in political struggle

Malnutrition   Lack of suitable body building foods

Mass   Word used by Roman Catholics to describe the service which remembers Jesus' last supper with his disciples

Messiah   The person expected by the Jews to help them and lead them. The word Messiah is Hebrew for 'anointed'

Missionary   Someone who is sent out by a Church with the job of telling others about Jesus

Multi-racial   A society with many different races.

Natural resources   The useful things which a country has, e.g. oil, coal, minerals

New Testament   The second part of the Bible

Non-violence   A refusal to act violently, whatever the provocation

Nuptial Mass   A service of Holy Communion held immediately after a marriage

Old Testament   The first part of the Christian Bible. Part of the Jewish scriptures

Outcast   Person despised and rejected by other social groups

Pacifism   A belief that war is totally wrong in every circumstance

Persecution   When someone is mistreated, imprisoned, tortured or discriminated against because of their beliefs.

Prejudice   Unreasonable treatment of others because of their colour, nationality, gender, age, etc.

Priest   In Orthodox, Catholic and Anglican traditions, a priest is someone set apart by the Church to do the work which Jesus gave to his disciples

Prophet   Person who proclaims the word of God for their own times

Protestant   Churches, or Christians, who are not Roman Catholic or Orthodox

Quakers   A group of Christians also called the Society of Friends

Race   Ethnic origin of people, e.g. the African race, the Slavonic race

Reformation   16th century movement which resulted in the formation the Protestant Church

Reformers   People who wish to change either the Church or social conditions

Refugee   A person who has been forced to flee from their own country because they are in danger from persecution, famine or war

Regime   Government

Register   Add new babies to the list of people in Britain

Registrar   A person authorized to record births and deaths, and to marry people

Register office   A place where births and deaths are recorded, and where some people choose to get married

Sabbath   The seventh day, on which working was forbidden

Sacrament   An act of worship, rite, or ceremony, with a deeper meaning, as a sign of grace

Segregation   The division of society according to people's race

Slave trade   Selling people

Stewardship   Careful control of time, talents, money, and looking after the earth

Third World   The poorer, developing countries of the south

Vocation   A sense of calling to a particular task in life

Voluntary work   Work done to help the community, usually unpaid

Volunteer   Someone who has chosen to perform a task, usually unpaid